Great Misadventures

Great Misadventures
Bad Ideas That Led to Big Disasters

PEGGY SAARI
EDITED BY BETZ DES CHENES

VOLUME FOUR: SOCIETY

U·X·L®
AN IMPRINT OF GALE

Detroit • London

Great Misadventures:
Bad Ideas That Led to Big Disasters
Peggy Saari

Staff

Elizabeth Des Chenes, *U·X·L Senior Editor*
Carol DeKane Nagel, *U·X·L Managing Editor*
Thomas L. Romig, *U·X·L Publisher*

Margaret Chamberlain, *Permissions Specialist (Pictures)*

Mary Beth Trimper, *Production Director*
Evi Seoud, *Assistant Production Manager*
Deborah Milliken, *Production Assistant*

Cynthia Baldwin, *Product Design Manager*
Michelle Dimercurio, *Art Director*
Linda Mahoney, *Typesetting*

Library of Congress Cataloging-in-Publication Data

Great Misadventures: Bad Ideas That Led to Big Disasters/ Peggy Saari, editor
   v. cm.
   Includes bibliographical references.
   Summary: Explores 100 historical, political, military, and social events
where human error has led to disaster.
   ISBN 0-7876-2798-4 (set: alk. paper). — ISBN 0-7876-2799-2 (v. 1: alk.
paper) — ISBN 0-7876-2800-X (v. 2: alk. paper) — ISBN 0-7876-2801-8 (v. 3:
alk paper) — ISBN 0-7876-2802-6 (v. 4: alk. paper)
   1. History—Miscellanea—Juvenile literature. 2. Disasters—Juvenile literature. [1. Disasters. 2. History—Miscellanea]
   I. Saari, Peggy.
   D24 G64 1998
   904—dc21   98-13811
                                                                             CIP

Contents

VOLUME THREE: MILITARY

Reader's Guide

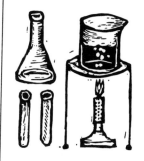

Great Misadventures: Bad Ideas That Led to Big Disasters presents 100 stories of human error, greed, and poor judgment that span history from ancient times through the present. Each entry, whether on an infamous adventure, a technological failure, a deadly battle, or a social calamity, offers historical background and a vivid description of the event, together with a discussion about why the misadventure is significant.

In many cases, a misadventure had a positive outcome—laws were enacted, failure led to progress, the protagonist became a national hero—but in others, death or destruction were the only result. It is disillusioning to learn, for example, that a great explorer committed atrocities, or that a well-known celebrity was a liar. It is equally disturbing to discover that incompetent leaders caused needless loss of life in wars, or that cutting-edge technology was sometimes useless or even dangerous. The goal of Great Misadventures is to show that success can also involve failure, triumph can encompass defeat, and human beings are inspired by self-interest as often as they are motivated by selflessness.

Format

The Great Misadventures entries are arranged chronologically within four subject volumes: Exploration and Adventure, Science and Technology, Military, and Society. Cross references direct users to related entries throughout the four-volume set, while sources for further reference at the end of each entry offer more information on featured people and events. Call-out boxes present biographical profiles and fascinating facts, and more than 220 black-and-white photographs, illustrations, and

maps help illuminate the text. Each volume contains an anno-
tated table of contents, a timeline of important events, and a
cumulative index.

Comments and Suggestions

We welcome your comments and suggestions for subjects
to feature in future editions of *Great Misadventures*. Please
write: Editors, *Great Misadventures,* U•X•L, 27500 Drake Rd.,
Farmington Hills, Michigan, 48331–3535; call toll-free:
800–877–4253; or fax 1–800–414–5043.

Timeline

415 B.C. Athenian naval commander Alcibiades is defeated during an assault on Syracuse.

325 B.C. Macedonian leader Alexander the Great leads a tragic expedition across the Gedrosia desert.

30 B.C. Egyptian queen Cleopatra commits suicide.

1118 French philosopher Peter Abelard begins a tragic love affair with his student Hëloise.

1187 Christian Crusaders lose the Battle of Hattin to the Muslims.

1212 Stephen of Cloyes, a French shepherd boy, leads the ill-fated Children's Crusade.

1498 Italian explorer Christopher Columbus begins his rule of Hispaniola.

c. 1500 The Norse settlement in Greenland is abandoned.

1533 Spanish conquistador Pedro de Alvarado leads a disastrous trek across the Andes.

1541 Spanish conquistador Francisco Vázquez de Coronado fails to find the Seven Cities of Cibola.

214 B.C
Great Wall of
China is built

1215
Magna Carta
is written

1455
War of the Roses
begins

250 B.C. 1100 1300 1500

1591 English colonists disappear from the Roanoke settlement.

1597 Dutch explorer Willem Barents dies in a failed attempt to find a northeast sea passage to Asia.

1605 English Roman Catholics fail to blow up Parliament as part of the Gunpowder Plot.

1618 English explorer Sir Walter Raleigh is beheaded for disobeying King James I.

1625 The British fleet is defeated in a disastrous misadventure at the port of Cádiz, Spain.

1687 French explorer René-Robert de La Salle is killed by his own men.

1709 The Swedish army loses the Battle of Poltava because of a squabble between two of its commanders.

1776 Hessian colonel Johann Gottlieb Rall loses the Battle of Trenton when he underestimates rebel troop strength.

1779 English explorer James Cook is murdered by angry Hawaiian islanders.

1806 Scottish explorer Mungo Park drowns during an expedition on the Niger River.

1811 Rebellious English textile workers calling themselves "Luddites" begin a failed uprising against the Industrial Revolution.

1812 Poor leadership by American general William Hull leads to the Fall of Detroit during the War of 1812.

1815 French leader Napoléon Bonaparte is defeated by British forces at the Battle of Waterloo.

1831 African American slave Nat Turner leads the failed Southampton Insurrection.

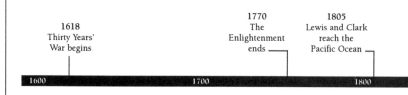

1618
Thirty Years'
War begins

1770
The
Enlightenment
ends

1805
Lewis and Clark
reach the
Pacific Ocean

1600   1700   1800

1844 Canadian trapper Peter Skene Ogden explores territory for Britain that is later lost to the United States in a land dispute.

1846 Donner Party members resort to cannibalism after being trapped in the Sierra Nevada.

1847 British explorer John Franklin is lost at sea during his search for the Northwest Passage.

1855 Deprivations during the Crimean War lead to an overwhelming number of deaths among British soldiers.

1859 Abolitionist John Brown stages a failed raid on the federal arsenal at Harpers Ferry, Virginia.

1861 Australian explorers Robert O'Hara Burke and William John Wills starve to death during their transcontinental expedition.

1863 Confederate general George Edward Pickett marches his troops to certain death at the Battle of Gettysburg.

1863 The African American 54th Massachusetts Regiment stages an heroic but unsuccessful assault on Fort Wagner, South Carolina.

1870 Paraguay's male population is reduced by almost ninety percent during the "War of the Triple Alliance."

1873 British missionary and explorer David Livingstone dies during his final adventure in Africa.

1873 French explorer Francis Garnier makes a tactical error that ends French control of the Vietnamese city of Hanoi.

1876 The 7th Cavalry is annihilated by Sioux and Cheyenne warriors at the Battle of Little BigHorn.

1881 American explorer George Washington De Long and his crew are lost while attempting to find a route to the North Pole through the Bering Strait.

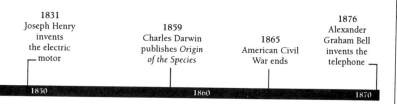

1831
Joseph Henry invents the electric motor

1859
Charles Darwin publishes *Origin of the Species*

1865
American Civil War ends

1876
Alexander Graham Bell invents the telephone

1850   1860   1870

1908 American explorer Frederick Albert Cook claims to be the first man to reach the North Pole.

1911 One hundred and forty-six immigrant workers perish in the Triangle Shirtwaist Company fire in New York City.

1912 British explorer Robert Falcon Scott and his party freeze to death on their return trip from the South Pole.

1912 The luxury ocean liner *Titanic* sinks after hitting an iceberg.

1915 Poor leadership and bad communication leads to high Allied casualties at the Battle of Gallipoli.

1916 Irish revolutionaries stage the unsuccessful Easter Rising.

1919 A steel tank containing 12,000 tons of molasses bursts open in Boston, Massachusetts, and kills twenty-one people.

1919 British troops kill 379 unarmed Indian protestors during the Amritsar Massacre.

1920 Seven Chicago White Sox players are banned from playing baseball for their role in the "Black Sox" betting scandal.

1928 Italian pilot Umberto Nobile crashes the airship *Italia* during a flight to the North Pole.

1934 The Dionne quintuplets are born in Canada and soon become a tourist and media attraction.

1937 American aviator Amelia Earhart and her navigator Fred Noonan are lost on a flight across the Pacific Ocean.

1937 The airship *Hindenberg* explodes after landing in Lakehurst, New Jersey.

1938 The *War of the Worlds* radio broadcast about a fictional Martian invasion causes widespread public panic.

1902 Cuba achieves independence	1914 World War I begins	1929 Great Depression begins
1900	1910	1920	1930

1941 German leader Adolf Hitler launches Operation Barbarossa, his failed invasion of Russia.

1944 The Japanese navy and air force stage a futile kamikaze attack at the Battle of Leyte Gulf.

1947 American inventor Howard Hughes flies his *Spruce Goose* seaplane for ninety seconds.

1950 U.S. senator Joseph McCarthy launches his four-year search for Communist infiltrators.

1951 U.S. general Douglas MacArthur is relieved of his command during the Korean War.

1953 Julius and Ethel Rosenberg become the first U.S. citizens to be executed for espionage.

1956 A United Airlines DC-7 and a TWA Constellation collide in empty air space over the Grand Canyon.

1956 American college instructor Charles Van Doren becomes involved in the *Twenty-One* quiz show scandal.

1961 CIA-trained Cuban refugees fail to overthrow dictator Fidel Castro during the Bay of Pigs invasion.

1961 The U.S. Air Force begins spraying the defoliant Agent Orange in Vietnam.

1969 General Motors discontinues production of the controversial Chevrolet Corvair, America's first rear-engine automobile.

1970 American astronauts abort the *Apollo 13* mission to the Moon.

1972 A failed burglary at the offices of the Democratic National Committee sets the stage for the Watergate scandal.

1973 The United States ends its long and disastrous military involvement in the Vietnam War.

1939–45
World War II

1950
Korean War
begins

1962
Cuban missile
crisis

1965–73
The Vietnam
War

1940   1950   1960   1970

1978 The Ford Motor Company recalls 1.4 million Pinto automobiles after several fatal rear-impact collisions.

1979 The Three Mile Island nuclear power plant in Pennsylvania has an accidental meltdown.

1980 Love Canal, New York, is evacuated after years of toxic waste dumping make this residential area uninhabitable.

1980 Fire protection systems fail to prevent a blaze from engulfing the MGM Grand Hotel in Las Vegas, Nevada.

1980 U.S. military forces stage an aborted rescue of American hostages in Tehran, Iran.

1983 Artificial heart recipient Barney Clark dies 112 days after his historic surgery.

1983 The infamous copper mining "Pit" in Butte, Montana is closed.

1984 A poisonous gas cloud escapes from the Union Carbide chemical plant in Bhopal, India, killing thousands of people.

1986 Two mammoth explosions blow apart Unit 4 of the Chernobyl nuclear power plant in the Ukraine.

1986 The entire flight crew dies when the space shuttle *Challenger* explodes after launch.

1989 The oil tanker Exxon *Valdez* runs aground in Alaska, spilling 10.8 million gallons of crude oil and polluting 1,500 miles of shoreline.

1991 U.S. diplomatic failures help trigger the Persian Gulf War.

1992 Silicone breast implants are banned by the Food and Drug Administration.

1992 John Gotti, the "Teflon Don," is sentenced to life in prison after his underboss, Sammy "the Bull" Gravano, testifies against the Gambino crime family.

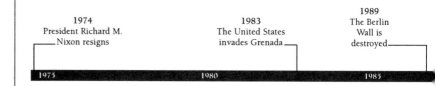

1974
President Richard M.
Nixon resigns

1983
The United States
invades Grenada

1989
The Berlin
Wall is
destroyed

1975   1980   1985

1992 American adventurer Christopher McCandless starves to death during an Alaskan wilderness trek.

1993 The U.S. Congress ends funding for the Superconductor Super Collider.

1994 U.S. figure skater Tanya Harding is implicated in an assault on fellow skater Nancy Kerrigan.

1994 CIA agent Aldrich Ames is convicted of spying for the Soviet Union.

1995 Twelve people die and thousands are injured in a nerve gas attack in Tokyo, Japan.

1995 English stock trader Nicholas Leeson triggers the collapse of Barings PLC.

1995 The controversial Denver International Airport in Colorado finally opens for business.

1996 The British government orders the slaughter of thousands of cattle infected with mad cow disease.

1996 Seven-year-old American pilot Jessica Dubroff dies while trying to set an aviation record.

1996 Seven climbers perish during a blizzard on Mount Everest.

1997 The MRTA hostage crisis at the Japanese embassy in Lima, Peru, reaches a violent climax.

1997 The Canadian Bre-X mining company is shut down after the world's largest "gold discovery" proves to be a hoax.

1997 American scientist Karen Wetterhahn dies after being exposed to liquid mercury during a laboratory experiment.

1998 Federal Aviation Administration technicians conclude that the mainframe computer used in the nation's largest air traffic control centers is "Year 2000" compliant.

1992
Los Angeles
riots

1995
Yitzhak Rabin
is assassinated

1998
President
Bill Clinton
visits China

1990   1995   2000

Great Misadventures

Cleopatra's Fall

30 B.C

Cleopatra (69 B.C.–30 B.C.) was the last Ptolemy queen of Egypt and one of the best-known romantic heroines in history. Although she was perhaps not beautiful by modern standards, Cleopatra had great personal charm, an appeal that she used to further her political ambitions. Using little more than her great persuasive skills, Cleopatra tried to reestablish the power of the Egyptian empire after it had fallen under Roman rule. As the mistress of the Roman dictator Julius Caesar and then the wife of Roman emperor Marc Antony, Cleopatra's manipulation of people and events ultimately led to her own undoing. Her schemes also brought an end to the Ptolemaic dynasty in Egypt.

Becomes queen of Egypt

In 51 B.C., at the age of seventeen, Cleopatra ascended the Egyptian throne as Cleopatra VIII. According to ancient custom, she had married her younger brother, Ptolemy XII (c. 61? B.C.–47 B.C.), who was only ten. Ptolemy had succeeded his deceased father, Ptolemy XI (112 B.C.–51 B.C.), as monarch. Because Ptolemy was a minor, he ruled with the assistance of a three-person regency council. Immediately perceiving the strong-willed Cleopatra as a threat, the council deposed her (removed her from the throne). Cleopatra fled to Syria, raised

> "The charm of her presence was irresistible, and there was an attraction in her person and her talk ... [that] laid all who associated with her under its spell."
>
> —Roman historian Plutarch

Cleopatra (far right) was the last Ptolemy queen of Egypt. She was also the mistress of Roman dictator Julius Caesar and the wife of soldier-statesman Marc Antony.

an army, and returned to Alexandria (the capital of Egypt) ready to do battle against Ptolemy and his council.

In 48 B.C. Julius Caesar (100 B.C.–44 B.C.), the dictator of Rome, arrived at Alexandria with a small force of soldiers. He declared that Cleopatra's father had left a will putting the welfare of his royal children in the hands of the Roman Senate. By this reasoning, Caesar settled the dispute between Cleopatra and her brother. The council agreed to this arrangement, confident that they would be able to assassinate Cleopatra if she tried to enter Alexandria. Unable to enter the city safely, Cleopatra sent a large carpet to Caesar as a gift. When it was unrolled, Caesar—who was fifty-two years old at the time—was astonished and delighted to find the beautiful young queen wrapped inside it. The couple reportedly became lovers that same night.

Bears Caesar's son

Despite his infatuation with Cleopatra, Caesar proposed that she and Ptolemy resume their joint rule. This suggestion did not satisfy Ptolemy's advisors, who surrounded the city with troops. When Roman reinforcements arrived, Caesar decisively defeated the Egyptian force. Ptolemy drowned while trying to escape. Caesar then arranged for Cleopatra to marry her other brother, Ptolemy XIII (died 44 B.C.), and made the siblings joint rulers. Cleopatra also became Caesar's "official" mistress. According to Roman historian Plutarch (A.D 46–A.D. 20), Cleopatra bore Caesar his only son, a child named Caesarion (later Ptolemy XIV). While some historians have disputed Caesarion's parentage, Cleopatra always insisted that Caesarion was Caesar's child. She hoped that her son would one day inherit Caesar's powerful position as dictator of Rome.

In 46 B.C., Cleopatra traveled to Rome, apparently to participate in Caesar's enormous Triumph, a parade and celebration of his victories in Egypt, North Africa, and Gaul (present-day France). Caesar dedicated a new temple to the Roman goddess Venus and placed a statue of Cleopatra inside it. He also made Cleopatra a member of his family, an act that scandalized Rome. (In Roman society, citizenship was a sacred honor not lightly conferred on foreigners.) Caesar also gave his mistress a country home outside Rome, offending his virtuous wife Calpurnia and further scandalizing Roman citizens.

Rumors soon began to fly saying that Caesar planned to move the capital of the empire from Rome to Alexandria. On March 15, 44 B.C., however, Caesar was assassinated by republicans who feared he would establish a monarchy with himself as king. Caesar's will proclaimed Octavian (63 B.C.–A.D. 14), his nephew and adopted son, as the heir to the throne instead of Cleopatra's son. Cleopatra quickly fled by ship back to Alexandria, where she had her brother-husband Ptolemy murdered.

CLEOPATRA Cleopatra (69 B.C.–30 B.C.) was the daughter of the Egyptian monarch Ptolemy XI. She was the eighth and last in the line of Egyptian queens who bore the name Cleopatra. According to ancient custom, she married two of her brothers, Ptolemy XII and Ptolemy XIII, with whom she jointly ruled Egypt. When her country was conquered by Rome, she set out to restore the Ptolemy dynasty (family of rulers). A strong and charismatic woman, Cleopatra commanded fleets in important sea battles and gave birth to the only natural son of Roman dictator Julius Caesar. She was both loved and despised by Egyptians and Romans alike. Roman historian Plutarch once offered this description of Cleopatra: "The charm of her presence was irresistible, and there was an attraction in her person and her talk, together with a peculiar force of character which pervaded her every word and action, and laid all who associated with her under its spell."

Cleopatra's remarkable life has been the subject of numerous books, plays, films, and poems. Among them are the tragedy *Caesar and Cleopatra* by the British playwright William Shakespeare and a comedy of the same title by British playwright and critic George Bernard Shaw. At least two Hollywood films have been based on Cleopatra's story. The best known is *Cleopatra* (1963), which starred Elizabeth Taylor in the title role, with Richard Burton as Marc Antony. While the movie was being made, the actors' tempestuous relationship often rivaled that of Antony and Cleopatra.

Marries Marc Antony

Meanwhile, Octavian and Marc Antony (c. 81 B.C–30 B.C.), Caesar's friend and lieutenant, agreed to share the ruling of the empire with Lepidus (died c. 13 B.C.), another powerful Roman. The three men became known as the "second triumvirate." (The term "triumvirate" refers to a rule by three, in this case, three men.) In 42 B.C. Antony won a glorious victory at Philippi in Greece that effectively put him in control of the Roman Empire.

Shortly after this victory Antony requested that Cleopatra, who was now twenty-eight years old, meet him at Tarsus (in present-day Turkey) to answer charges that she had helped the enemies of the second triumvirate. Historians speculate that Cleopatra had designs on trying to regain the Egyptian throne through Antony. She arrived at Tarsus in an enormous, gilded barge decorated to look like an enchanted forest. Cleopatra immediately charmed Antony, just as she had charmed Caesar. Antony then spent years in idle luxury at Cleopatra's side while the security of Rome's eastern provinces deteriorated.

When Octavian eventually managed to gain the upper hand, Antony hastily left Egypt for Rome.

In 40 B.C., Octavian and Antony agreed to a power-sharing arrangement that made Antony ruler of the eastern part of the Roman Empire. Octavian took Rome and the western provinces. To cement the agreement, Antony married Octavian's half-sister Octavia. In 37 B.C. Antony left Rome, taking Octavia only as far as Greece. He then summoned Cleopatra to meet him at Antioch (in present-day Turkey). Antony and Cleopatra were married in a ritual that was recognized in the eastern territories but not in Rome. Antony named Cleopatra ruler of all the territories formerly held by her ancestors, the Ptolemaic rulers of Egypt. She later bore him several children, including Alexander, Helios, and Cleopatra Selene.

Marc Antony, along with Octavian and Lepidus, formed the "second triumvirate" that shared rule over Rome.

Loses battle of Actium

Antony's infatuation with Cleopatra seemed to impair his abilities both as a military commander and as a ruler. He lost important battles and bestowed countries he had not yet conquered on Cleopatra and her children. In 32 B.C., he formally divorced Octavia and ordered her to leave his house in Rome, even though she had been faithfully caring for their children. In response, Octavian declared war on Cleopatra and called Antony an agent of a foreign state.

The following year Antony and Cleopatra assembled their ships and armies for a confrontation with Octavian near the town of Actium in Greece. Although the couple's forces were superior in numbers, Octavian had the brilliant general Agrippa (c. 63 B.C.–12 B.C.). Antony's fleet was soon blockaded on the Ambracian Gulf (an inlet of the Ionian Sea on the west coast of Greece). The battle lasted only a few minutes, and the fleet was quickly destroyed. Recognizing defeat, Cleopatra's ships raised their sails and headed for Egypt. Antony then abandoned his fleet and land troops—the most serious offense a Roman commander could commit—and chased after Cleopatra's ship in a small, swift galley (a ship propelled by oars). Now a broken man, he returned to Alexandria with Cleopatra. Antony's abandoned ship crews and the various princes of the eastern empire pledged their allegiance to Octavian.

Betrays Antony?

Both Antony and Cleopatra appealed to Octavian for mercy. Octavian replied only to Cleopatra, saying that if she would expel Antony from Egypt, she could ask for anything. Cleopatra refused. Finally, in 30 B.C., Antony and his army faced Octavian and his forces outside Alexandria. On the day of the battle, both Egypt's navy and Antony's own forces deserted to Octavian's side. Antony rode back to Alexandria, convinced that Cleopatra had betrayed him. Fearing his anger, Cleopatra fled to her royal tomb. When Antony was told that his wife had died, he tried to commit suicide by falling on his sword, a time-honored Roman custom. Mortally injured, he was carried to Cleopatra's tomb, where he later died in her arms.

Octavian's soldiers managed to penetrate Cleopatra's stronghold and took her prisoner. Although Octavian promised not to harm her, he actually planned to take her to Rome, no doubt to appear in chains at his Triumph. In one last act of desperation, Cleopatra grabbed an asp (a poisonous snake) that was hidden in a basket of figs. She then wrote a letter to Octavian, begging for mercy for her children. By the time he received the letter, she had put the asp to her throat and killed herself. With Cleopatra's death came an end to the Ptolemaic line of rulers. Egypt then became Rome's "bread basket" and one of many exploited provinces in the Roman Empire. Octavian went on to a long reign as the celebrated Emperor Augustus. It would be centuries before Egypt was again ruled by Egyptians.

FOR FURTHER REFERENCE

Books

Brooks, Polly Schroyer. *Cleopatra: Goddess of Egypt, Enemy of Rome*. New York City: HarperCollins, 1995.

Stanley, Diane. *Cleopatra*. New York City: Morrow Junior Books, 1994.

The Romance of Héloïse and Abelard

1118

The letters of Héloïse and Abelard, which give a moving testament of their tragic love, are still famous today.

The tragic romance between Héloïse and Peter Abelard is one of the best-known love stories in history. Abelard was a theologian and philosopher who was entrusted with educating Héloïse. The two fell in love, had a son, and were secretly married. Héloïse's uncle did not approve of the union, however, so he had Abelard attacked and castrated. Abelard then became a monk while Héloïse entered a convent to escape the gossip surrounding the couple's controversial relationship. Abelard later gave property to the nuns associated with Héloïse when their convent was closed. Héloïse eventually became a successful abbess. The letters Héloïse and Abelard wrote to one another during their separation became legendary. Since the late eighteenth century the lovers' bodies have rested side by side at Pere-Lachaise cemetery in Paris, France.

Héloïse and Abelard fall in love

When Abelard met Héloïse he was a well-known theologian (religious thinker) and philosopher. Abelard had recently studied theology in the cathedral school at Laon, northeast of Paris. His teacher was the elderly Anselm of Laon, the most renowned master of this subject. After a time, however, Abelard found Anselm's teaching shallow and boring. In response to the urging of his fellow students, he began lectur-

567

ing on the scriptures of Ezekiel. This caused a breach with Anselm, and Abelard was expelled from Laon. In 1113 he returned to the cathedral school in Paris, where he had taught earlier. Abelard continued his teaching career for a number of years in relative peace.

By mutual agreement with Fulbert, a canon (clergyman) at the cathedral in Paris, Abelard then went to live at Fulbert's house. He was hired as the tutor of Fulbert's young, cultured, and beautiful niece Héloïse. Abelard and Héloïse soon fell in love. After several months, Fulbert discovered the couple's affair and forced Abelard to leave. At this time Abelard was about forty years old and Héloïse about eighteen years old.

Lovers have son and marry

Héloïse then discovered that she was pregnant. With Abelard's cooperation she left Paris in order to have the child in the more secluded and secure surroundings of Le Pallet, where Abelard's relatives lived. She gave birth to a son, Astralabe, who was left with Abelard's sister. Héloïse returned to Paris soon afterward, and she and Abelard married at the insistence of Fulbert. Héloïse was outraged by the couple's forced union, for she believed that the marriage was a disgrace. Not only would it destroy Abelard's career in the church, but it went against the lovers' belief that man is set apart from human ties. To protect

Abelard's church career and his reputation as a committed philosopher, the marriage initially was to remain a secret. Fulbert, however, was concerned about his own reputation and that of his niece. He eventually broke his promise, openly acknowledging Abelard as his nephew-in-law.

Enter the monastic life

Fulbert was furious when he learned that Abelard and Héloïse were still concealing their marriage. In order to protect Héloïse, Abelard sent his wife to the convent (a religious organization for women) at Argenteuil and made her wear a postulant's habit (the distinctive dress of a young woman who is preparing to become a nun) at all times. Abelard's move made Fulbert even angrier. He thought Abelard was seeking to annul (cancel) the marriage by forcing Héloïse into the religious life. Fulbert therefore hired men to seize Abelard while he slept and castrate him (remove his testicles).

The crime resulted in the disgrace of Fulbert and the death of the men who had attacked Abelard. More importantly, it brought a temporary end to Abelard's teaching career. Both he and Héloïse adopted the monastic life, she at Argenteuil and he at St. Denis, the famous Benedictine monastery (Roman Catholic religious order for men) north of Paris. At first Héloïse was not committed to the religious life. She had been with Abelard for eighteen months, and was just nineteen years old when she gave up her life outside the convent walls. Only later, through the famous letters between the tragic lovers, was the depth of Héloïse's unhappiness revealed.

Abelard's life at St. Denis was equally difficult. The castration had caused him public humiliation and exposed his affair with Héloïse. He was also separated from the cathedral schools and subjected to the authority of an abbot (head of a monastery), which was a new and unpleasant experience for him. Nevertheless, Abelard's reputation attracted students and his abbot permitted him to set up a school in a daughter priory (religious house for women) near the monastery.

Abelard resumes career

The resumption of Abelard's teaching career brought criticism from his rivals. His most vocal critics were Alberic and

Lotulf of Rheims, who maintained that a monk should not teach philosophy. They also claimed that Abelard's training in theology was insufficient. They specifically attacked a work on the Trinity (a Christian doctrine relating to God, Christ, and the Holy Spirit) that Abelard had written for his students at St. Denis. Alberic in particular was instrumental in calling a council at Soissons in 1121, which condemned Abelard's work. Abelard was also placed under "house arrest," first at St. Medard and then at St. Denis. Additional friction with his fellow monks forced Abelard to flee to a priory affiliated with St. Denis in Provins. The priory was located in the territory of the Count of Chartres, who was friendly toward him.

In spite of these reversals, Abelard still found time to write instructional materials for his students. His most famous work, *Sic et non* ("Yes and No"), appears to have been written in this period. It was intended as an instructional guide for students debating theological questions. In the work Abelard placed conflicting quotations from earlier Christian thinkers side by side, and he indicated the procedures the student should follow in arriving at a solution to the problems. Abelard did not attack traditional views, but he suggested that reliance on authority should be combined with critical thinking.

Héloïse heads Paraclete

In 1122 the abbot of St. Denis allowed Abelard to found a primitive hermitage (an isolated monastery) on a piece of land between Provins and Troyes. There he built a school and church, which he dedicated to the Paraclete (Holy Spirit). This period of quiet teaching away from the centers of civilization was interrupted in 1125. Abelard was opposed by Norbert of Premontre and Bernard of Clairvaux, representatives of a new type of piety (religious devotion). Seeking the safety of his boyhood home, Abelard returned to Brittany. He was appointed abbot of the unruly monastery of St. Gildas, on the coast near Vannes. For ten years Abelard struggled to bring order to the monastery.

Abelard was also able to spend time with Héloïse, whom he now called "my sister in Christ rather than my wife." She

◄Héloïse and Abelard are one of the most famous couples in history. The lovers' letters to each other reflect both their romantic past and philosophical issues of the day.

and her fellow nuns had been expelled from Argenteuil by the abbot of St. Denis. Abelard then deeded the hermitage of the Paraclete to them, and Héloïse became the abbess (head of a religious order for women). During Héloïse's lifetime Paraclete grew to be one of the most distinguished religious houses in France. Eventually six daughter houses were founded to take over the increasing number of postulants. Héloïse's superior administrative abilities were instrumental in the success of Paraclete, and she was remembered fondly for her work there.

Write famous letters

Abelard and Héloïse were again parted, this time permanently. Héloïse was later introduced to the *Historia calamitatum,* Abelard's autobiography in the form of a letter. Héloïse then wrote to Abelard, beginning an exchange of letters that eventually became famous. Because the couple had been apart for so long, the sentiments they expressed were heart wrenching. Héloïse's suffering over human love is especially apparent. In her first letter she expressed dismay over Abelard's description of his misfortunes and said she feared for his life. She also voiced her resentment over his attitude toward the sacrifice she made by entering the convent, as he knew she did so only out of love for him. She had no choice but to conclude, she wrote, that what he felt for her was only lust. Abelard answered naively that he had believed she no longer needed him after they took up the religious life. He also explained that he wanted to put the past behind him, and that he now was dedicated to God.

In another letter, Héloïse spoke of her sexual frustration and inability to forget their life as lovers. She felt she was being hypocritical because she took vows, not for the love of God, but also for her love of Abelard. Abelard then replied with irritation at her dredging up of old memories. He begged her to release her conflicted feelings and to think only of the love of Christ.

Héloïse forgets past

Eventually, Héloïse wrote to Abelard with dignity and self-control. Her writings focused on building a successful religious community, and she asked for her former lover's advice. Abelard responded with detailed information about running a convent. He also emphasized education, and many of his ideas

were the basis for the rules later adhered to at Paraclete. The
couple's exchanges continued, many in the form of hymns and
lessons intended for the nuns of the order. Abelard always pref-
aced his messages with a note for Héloïse. Although the two
would never again have the contact Héloïse longed for, Abelard
taught his former student that they could be reunited in their
love of God.

Abelard excommunicated

In 1136 Abelard returned to Paris to teach at the church of
St. Geneviève. For the next four years, he continued to attract
students as well as opposition from Bernard and others. During this period Abelard wrote a work on ethics, which took as
its title *Know Thyself*, a quotation from the Greek philosopher
Socrates. In his book, Abelard stressed the importance of eval-
uating a person's intention before deciding the morality or
immorality of an act. By expressing this bold belief, Abelard
incurred the wrath of Bernard. As a result, church officials held
a second trial to determine whether Abelard was guilty of violating church orthodoxy (official teachings). A council con-

vened at Sens in 1140 resulted in the condemnation of Abelard, and he was excommunicated (expelled) from the church. Proclaiming his innocence, Abelard decided to present his case to the pope (head of the Roman Catholic Church) at the Vatican in Rome, Italy.

Reunited after death

Abelard began his journey to Italy, but illness forced him to stop in Burgundy at the Cluniac priory of St. Marcel near Chalon-sur-Saône. He was granted protection by his former pupil Peter the Venerable, Abbot of Cluny, who requested Abelard remain at Cluny during his retirement. Abelard died eighteen months later, on April 21, 1142. He was later buried at Paraclete. After Abelard's death, Héloïse exchanged letters with Peter. She thanked him for bringing Abelard back to Paraclete and asked him to make financial arrangements for their son, Astralabe. Héloïse died in 1163 or 1164, and she was buried beside Abelard at Paraclete. When Paraclete was destroyed after the French Revolution (1789–99; a violent movement to overthrow the monarchy and replace it with a democratic form of government), the couple's remains were moved to Père-Lachaise cemetery in Paris.

FOR FURTHER REFERENCE

Books

Ericson, Donald E. *Abelard and Héloïse: Their Lives, Their Love, Their Letters.* New York City: Bennett-Edwards, 1990.

Witchcraft Hysteria

1486 TO c. 1710

O n December 5, 1484, the Roman Catholic pope issued a papal bull (an official letter) called *Summis desiderantes,* which stated the need to root out heresy (religious opinion contrary to accepted church beliefs). To help stamp out heretical thought, the pope appointed two German Dominicans, Henry Krämer (who later Latinized his name to Intitoris) and Jacob Sprenger, as inquisitors (official church examiners). As part of their task, the two men wrote a book called *Malleus Maleficarum* ("The Hammer of Witches"), which was published in 1486. The ideas presented in the *Malleus Maleficarum* contributed to a witchcraft hysteria that swept through Europe beginning in the fifteenth century. This frenzy eventually made its way to Salem, Massachusetts, in the 1650s. As the hysteria grew in strength, tens of thousands of people—mostly women—were tried or executed for practicing witchcraft.

Witchcraft

The practice of witchcraft in Europe was rooted in pre-Christian, pagan cults that worshipped nature and recognized more than one god. Early pagan believers held that good and evil were equally powerful forces in the world, but later pagan worshippers rejected good as being false and misleading. At

The publication of the *Malleus Maleficarum* led to the persecution, arrest, torture, and execution of thousands of people suspected of practicing witchcraft.

one time, scholars thought only church and government authorities used accusations of witchcraft as a convenient way to persecute people who did not conform to established social norms. More recently, anthropologists (scientists who study human cultures) have taken a new perspective on the witchcraft hysteria of 1486 to 1700. These researchers see the witch-hunts as part of a common pattern of demonization (seeing people as a source of evil) that can be traced throughout human history, even into contemporary times.

Scholars make a distinction between sorcerers and witches. A sorcerer gains powers through study and initiation into a group. This is the practice that was attacked during the 1486 to 1700 witchcraft hysteria. By contrast, a witch inherits special powers. A twentieth-century example of witchcraft is Wicca (also called neo-paganism), which has no connection with sorcery. Followers of Wicca revere nature, worship a fertility goddess, advocate free living, and practice group healing. According to Wicca, Satan is a false creation of Christianity that has nothing to do with genuine paganism as it was practiced in pre-Christian times.

Book causes hysteria

The *Malleus Maleficarum* was an encyclopedia of contemporary knowledge about witches, as well as a handbook of methods for investigating the crime of witchcraft. While acknowledging that both men and women could be tempted by the devil to use magical powers to commit evil deeds, the authors maintained that women were the most at risk. The men backed their views with biblical, theological, historical, and anecdotal evidence. According to Krämer and Sprenger, women were more vulnerable because they were more superstitious, more sexually insatiable, more vain, and more clever than men. Pacts with the devil, the writers said, were sealed by sexual intercourse. Then witches were empowered to harm in many ways. They could cause storms, slay farm animals, kill infants in the womb, make women barren (unable to have children), and deprive men of their "virile members."

The last part of the book described how to accuse, question (using torture), sentence, and execute witches. Helping Krämer and Sprenger in their efforts, governments and church authorities throughout Europe—Protestant as well as

Catholic—increasingly passed laws and began criminal actions against witches. The concepts presented in the *Malleus Maleficarum* encouraged over two hundred years of witch-hunts that led to the persecution, arrest, torture, and execution of thousands of people.

Accusers use barbaric torture

The almost universal European persecution of witches reached its height between 1580 and 1660. Germany had the worst record, with authorities executing more than 3,000 women. Historical documents tell stories of horrendous deeds committed by overzealous government and religious officials intent on tracking down and annihilating suspected witches. During the early years of the Spanish Inquisition (a panel of inquiry established by the Roman Catholic Church for eradicating heresy), 100 people were burned daily as witches in a ritual called "auto-da-fé" (mass burning). Historical documents report that mass burnings had a carnival-like atmosphere, and spectators could buy food, souvenirs, and religious objects.

Beggars, vagabonds, and poor people were often targets of government campaigns to clean up society. For example, when the duke of Bavaria began his witchhunt in the early 1600s, Anna Pappenheimer, her husband Paul (a cleaner of latrines), their three sons, and two other people were arrested for witchcraft. On July 29, 1600, after submitting to torture, Anna and Paul Pappenheimer finally confessed to crimes such as flying on sticks, making magic potions, and causing storms. They also admitted to having intercourse with the devil, making pacts with the devil, and practicing dismemberment (the cutting up of bodies) and cannibalism (the consumption of human flesh).

The accused were also pressured into confessing to committing robberies, arson, and hundreds of murders. The Pappenheimers' punishment was carried out before thousands of onlookers, including the couple's eleven-year-old son (who was executed weeks later). First, officials ripped the couple's skin with red-hot pincers. Then the torturers tore off Anna's breasts and rubbed them around her mouth and her two older sons' mouths. Next the officials took the victims by cart in a procession for over half a mile to their place of execution. At the site, the men's limbs were broken on a large wheel. Finally, the Pappenheimers were tied to stakes and burned alive.

A witchcraft trial in Salem, Massachusetts, circa 1690. The witch-hunts that spread through Europe and New England often targeted poor people and citizens who did not conform to social norms of the day.

Frenzy spreads to New England

Within a half century witchcraft hysteria had reached the British colonies in New England. One of the best-known cases involved Anne Hibbins. On June 19, 1656, Massachusetts Bay Colony governor John Endecott (c. 1588–1665) sentenced Hibbins to "hang till she was dead" for practicing witchcraft. Approximately ten other people had been executed in New England before Hibbins, but her wealth made her situation unique. When Hibbins's husband William died in 1654, he left his wife a sizable estate. The couple had originally moved to the Bay Colony in the early 1630s. William became an upstanding citizen and was a magistrate (judge), a member of the Court of Assistants, a devout churchgoer, and a merchant. While William conformed to social norms, however, Anne refused to do so. She fought openly with men, thus angering many people in the community. The Boston Puritan church excommunicated (expelled) Anne in 1640. Because of her husband's standing in the colony, people tolerated Anne's behavior. His death, however, left her unprotected from her enemies, who tried, convicted, and executed her for witchcraft two years later.

In 1692 New England teenagers accused three women—Sarah Good, Sarah Osborne, and a Caribbean Indian slave named Tituba—of practicing witchcraft. Tituba was owned by the Paris family, which was headed by a prominent minister. The court did not sentence her to death because she confessed to many crimes of witchcraft and implicated others. Although Sarah Solart Poole Good was born into a well-to-do family, she and her second husband had suffered severe financial setbacks. By 1692 the couple was nearly destitute. From the start of the inquisition, Good staunchly denied allegations of witchcraft and tried to place guilt on Osborne. Good's husband suspected she was a witch and expressed his concerns. Authorities even arrested the Goods' four-year-old daughter, Dorcas, finally releasing her about eight months later. Thirty-eight-year-old Sarah Good was not so lucky. The court sentenced her to death and executed her. Sarah Osborne, who was sixty years old, also denied being a witch. She held a much higher social standing than either Good or Tituba, but that did not help her situation. She died in prison while awaiting trial.

Hysteria ends

The last regular trial for witchcraft in Western Europe took place in Glaris, a Protestant district of Switzerland. Anne Goeldi was accused by a local doctor of casting evil spells on his son. On June 17, 1782, Goeldi was found guilty and hanged. In the American colonies approximately forty people (mostly women) were executed for witchcraft by 1710, when the last trial in North America reportedly took place.

FOR FURTHER REFERENCE

Books

Kent, Deborah. *Salem Massachusetts.* New York City: Dillon Press, 1996.

Rice, Earle. *The Salem Witch Trials.* San Diego, CA: Lucent Books, 1997.

The Gunpowder Plot

NOVEMBER 5, 1605

On Guy Fawkes Day, bonfires are lit, fireworks are set off, and "Guys" are carried through the streets in England in memory of the Gunpowder Plot.

The Gunpowder Plot was a famous misadventure that took place on November 5, 1605, in London, England. The failed conspiracy gave rise to the English national holiday known as Guy Fawkes Day. The Gunpowder Plot was a scheme by a group of English Roman Catholics to blow up the British Parliament and to kill King James I; his wife, Queen Anne; and James's successor, Charles I. The plotters hoped that in the resulting chaos, Catholics would take over the country. The plot was masterminded by Robert Catesby, who enlisted the help of several fellow Catholics. The conspirators were angered by the lack of religious tolerance for Catholics in England, where Protestantism was the only religion condoned by the British government. The plotters' plan ended in disaster, however, after the news of the plot was leaked to government officials. The exposure of the conspiracy resulted in the conspirators' deaths and greatly worsened the situation for Catholics in England.

Repression of Catholics

After the death of Queen Elizabeth I (1533–1603), King James VI of Scotland ascended to the British throne as James I (1566–1625). During Elizabeth's rule, English Catholics were not free to practice their religion. It was a criminal offense to say or hear mass (the Catholic religious rite) or to be a priest. Catholics were also subject to heavy fines if they did not attend Anglican (Church of England) services. Catholicism remained alive, however, through the efforts of wealthy families who were able to pay the fines, and Jesuit priests who risked persecution and death. (Jesuits are members of the Roman Catholic Society of Jesus devoted to missionary and educational work).

King James breaks his promise

When James took the throne, Catholics were cautiously optimistic that there could be a change in the way they were treated. James I made political promises to the Catholics because his own mother, Mary, Queen of Scots, was Catholic and his wife, Anne of Denmark (1574–1619), was secretly a Catholic. It was James's failure to keep his word, however, that ignited the conspiracy known as the Gunpowder Plot. The plot was the brainstorm of Robert Catesby (1573–1605), a devout Catholic aristocrat. As the basis of his plan, Catesby used the

When James I assumed the English throne in 1603, he promised Catholics that they would have greater freedom to practice their religion.

Catholic teaching that, in some circumstances, tyrannicide (the killing of a tyrant) is justified. Catesby felt that the grave mistreatment of English Catholics demanded an extreme response. Many of Catesby's fellow Catholics did not agree with this reasoning. They believed that their faith—and patience—would help improve the situation.

Knowing that he could not carry out this mission on his own, Catesby enlisted the help of Thomas Winter, Thomas Percy (1560–1605), John Wright, and Guy Fawkes (1570–1606). A soldier who had recently returned from service in Flanders (a region in France), Fawkes would become the most famous conspirator in the Gunpowder Plot. In the spring of 1605, the group rented a cellar under the palace at Westminster, the home of the royal family. There, Fawkes hid twenty barrels of gunpowder. The men planned their assault to take place during the meeting of Parliament (the British legislative body) on November 5.

JAMES I The story of James I is a long saga of political intrigue and tragedy. James was the son of Mary, Queen of Scots (1542–1587) and Henry Stuart, Lord Darnley (1545–1567). In 1567 Mary was forced to abdicate (give up) the throne by her cousin, Queen Elizabeth I of England. At the age of one year, James became the king of Scotland, but he was placed under the care of noblemen until he was old enough to rule on his own. As James was growing up, he was caught in a political struggle between Catholics and Protestants. His mother was a Catholic, so her supporters favored a Scottish alliance with France (a Catholic country). Protestants, on the other hand, aligned themselves with Elizabeth, the English Protestant queen.

In 1582 James was taken prisoner by the Protestants, but he managed to escape a year later and began his Scottish reign as King James VI. At first, he sided with Catholic interests. When he decided that he wanted to become king of England, however, James switched his allegiance to the Protestants. In 1587 he approved Elizabeth's decision to behead his mother, Mary, Queen of Scots, thus ensuring his ascent to the English throne. When James arrived in England, he entered an even more intense political struggle. Although the Protestants controlled the country, they feared a Catholic takeover. Many suspected that James favored the Catholics because he was seeking an alliance with Spain (a Catholic country). To calm his critics, James strictly enforced laws prohibiting the practice of Catholicism. These actions led Catholic conspirators to devise the Gunpowder Plot.

The Gunpowder plot is diffused

Almost immediately the plan began to unravel. Catesby felt that he needed more help, so he decided to include Francis Tresham (c. 1567–1605) in the plot. This would prove to be Catesby's worst decision. Tresham warned his Catholic brother-in-law, Lord William Parker Monteagle (1575–1622), not to attend Parliament on November 5. Monteagle proceeded to alert the government about the conspiracy. Fawkes was discovered in the cellar, ready to ignite the gunpowder. He was tortured into revealing the identity of his cohorts.

Pursued into the Midlands (a region in central England), Catesby was killed in a shoot-out. Percy was killed while resisting arrest. The other conspirators were caught, imprisoned, and horribly executed. To compound the debacle, the government used this calamity to further incriminate Jesuit priests, who had not actually been involved in the plot. Several other guiltless Catholics were tried and executed in the scandal's aftermath.

VI SEPTEM NOBILIVM ANGLORVMCONIVRANTIVM IN NECEM IACOBI·I
MAGNÆ. BRITANNIÆ. REGIS TOTIVSQ. ANGLICI CONVOCATI PARLEMENTI·

Christopher Wright   Iohn Wright   Thomas Percy   Guido Fawkes   Robert Catesby   Thomas Winter

An engraving of the Gunpowder Plot conspirators. Robert Catesby (second from right) was the English Catholic aristocrat who devised an ill-fated plan to kill King James I and his family.

Guy Fawkes Day

Ultimately, the Gunpowder Plot only made the situation worse for English Catholics. Although the conspirators had intended to support the cause of their religion, the misadventure heightened government (and in many cases, public) hatred toward Catholics. Government officials resumed rigid enforcement of the recusancy law, which fined people who refused to attend Anglican services.

Although Fawkes had played a fairly insignificant role in the misadventure, he eventually became the most famous conspirator. In 1606, Parliament designated November 5 as a day of thanksgiving. Soon the holiday became known as "Guy Fawkes Day" in honor of Fawkes's role in the Gunpowder Plot. Even today, bonfires are lit, fireworks are set off, and "Guys" (dummies dressed up as Guy Fawkes) are carried through the streets of England on November 5.

FOR FURTHER REFERENCE

Books

Fraser, Antonia. *Faith and Treason: The Story of the Gunpowder Plot.* New York City: Doubleday, 1996.

The Luddite Movement

1811 TO 1816

Historians have generally taken an unfavorable view of the Luddites by portraying them as ignorant opponents of progress.

The Luddites were English textile workers who protested against the Industrial Revolution (a period of great technological development that lasted from the mid-1700s to the late 1800s). The Luddite movement began in 1811 around Nottingham, England. The Luddites embraced the anti-industrial tactics of a mythical hero named Ned Ludd, who allegedly destroyed factory machinery "by accident." Ludd's followers broke factory machinery deliberately in an effort to slow down technological progress and return to traditional methods of commerce. The Luddites supported the idea that self-reliance was an inalienable human right, and that men's livelihoods should never be dependent on—or replaced by—impersonal machines.

Even though the British government finally crushed the uprising in 1816, the followers of Ned Ludd were popular with the common people. As is evidenced by the rapid increase in mass production and technology during the nineteenth century, the early Luddite movement was a failure. Concerns about the negative effects of technology on human life and the environment, however, never died out. In fact, a new generation of Luddites called "neo-Luddites" became active in the 1990s.

A man with a sledgehammer destroys an English "spinning jenny." As part of their crusade against technology, the Luddites destroyed machinery in order to slow down or halt the mass production of goods.

The advent of machines

Before the Industrial Revolution began in England in the mid-1700s, apprenticeships (the passing of a skill or trade from one generation to the next) had been the method of learning and working for at least 300 years. Before the advent of mass industrialization, skilled workers were not employed in factories. They operated home workshops that were later given the name "cottage industries." In this system, families ran their own businesses, bought their own tools, and advertised their own wares.

After 1800 the development of certain machines, such as the power loom (a machine that manufactures fabric), began to threaten the traditional cottage businesses. As the Industrial Revolution progressed, rural craftsmen grew increasingly restless. They were unhappy for several reasons, but mainly because their products were being created by machines. One power loom, for instance, could do the work of several weavers. The machinery was too expensive for the ordinary craftsman, however, so production shifted to factory owners who could afford to buy many of the new inventions. Consequently, English workers moved from their home-based businesses into towns and cities.

Protections removed

Of all the small businesses that thrived in England before 1800, the weavers of Nottingham were the most prosperous. These craftsmen produced textiles (cloth), especially stockings and lace, which dominated both the domestic and foreign markets. The Nottingham craftsmen were protected by an old code called a royal charter that limited the production of certain kinds of textiles only to Nottingham and the surrounding area. The Luddite riots began in 1811 after the English government removed the restrictions of the royal charter and opened the textile market to factories throughout the country. This move threatened the livelihood of the Nottingham weavers, who had been able to support themselves modestly but comfortably under the old system. Now they were unable to afford the necessities of life, and they were angry.

Luddite movement begins

The story that sparked the Luddite revolution involved Ned Ludd, a young Nottingham weaver who may or may not have been an actual person. According to the tale, while Ned was working on a farm one day, he fell down and accidentally broke two frames that were used for making stockings. The frames' furious owner then scolded the poor young man. Whether or not Ned Ludd's actions were intentional, other workers saw the incident as a perfect way to fight against the Industrial Revolution. Calling themselves the Luddites, the rebels decided to imitate the actions of their young hero. Using sabotage (secret destruction) as their weapon against progress, the protesters would wreck the new machines and thus hold onto their old way of life.

At first, the Luddites were a secretive band of guerrillas (fighters who engage in tactics such as surprise attacks) who struck only at night and then retreated into the hills and forests around Nottingham. While the rebels used the legend of Ned Ludd as a symbol of revolt, they were also inspired by the French Revolution (1789–99; a movement in France that sought to overthrow the monarchy and establish a democratic

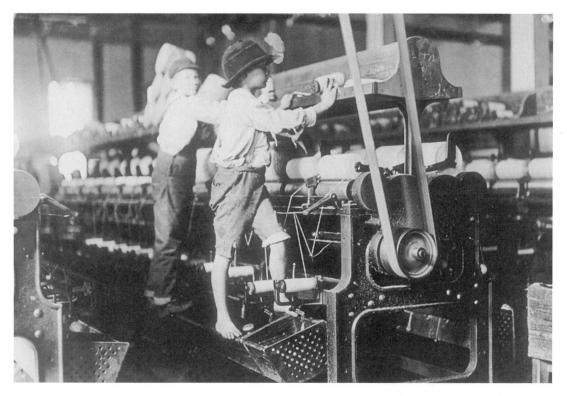

Two young boys at work in a nineteenth-century textile mill. As children were forced to take unsafe factory jobs, the average life expectancy in many areas dropped to eighteen years.

form of government). Another strong influence was American political thinker Thomas Paine (1737–1809), who argued in favor of individualism, human rights, and democracy.

When England became involved in the War of 1812 there was a widespread economic depression as soaring wheat prices drove up the cost of bread. (The War of 1812 was a conflict between the United States and Great Britain largely over land holdings and expansion in the American West.) The Luddite movement reached its peak in 1812 when workers mounted a series of full-scale and well-organized protests. Wearing disguises, the Luddites appeared at factories and announced that they had come on orders from "General Ned Ludd" or "King Ned Ludd." The attacks were not violent, and the Luddites wrecked only the machines of factory owners who did not meet their demands—they never harmed the owners or other workers. Soon the revolts spread from Nottingham to other regions such as Yorkshire, Derbyshire, Cheshire, and Leicestershire.

Government strikes back

Because the Luddites demanded higher wages and better working conditions, they were popular with local people. They also maintained their vow of nonviolence, and factory owners usually gave in to their demands. But the situation changed dramatically on April 20, 1812. That night over one thousand Luddites armed with sticks and rocks attacked Burton's power loom mill in Lancashire. After a private security force prevented the Luddites from entering the mill, they burned down the factory owner's house. The government then sent in soldiers, who killed several Luddites. Seeking revenge, the Luddites later murdered the factory owner.

In the aftermath of this incident, the government of Robert Banks Jenkinson, 2nd earl of Liverpool (1770–1858), held a mass trial in York. The following year many Luddites were convicted and imprisoned; fourteen people were hanged. This brutal effort at repression brought a temporary end to the Luddite movement. In 1816, during the economic depression that followed Britain's involvement in the Napoleonic Wars (1803–1815), the Luddites reemerged. On December 2, 1816, they struck at Spa Fields in London, only to be crushed once again by the government. In the decades following the Luddite riots, a third of England's population became destitute (poverty stricken). Because children were forced into labor, the life expectancy of the average worker was reduced to eighteen years, and fifty-seven percent of English children were dead before the age of five.

Twentieth-century Luddites

The Luddite movement could be dismissed as a failure if not for the fact that its ideas influenced later generations. Up through the late twentieth century, many people questioned the price of progress. Among these critics were neo-Luddites and other grassroots (small and independent) organizations. The neo-Luddites, for example, cite several technological and environmental disasters such as Three Mile Island and Love Canal (see "Science and Technology" entries) as evidence that technology takes an overwhelming toll on the Earth and humankind. The group also argues that reliance on computers in all aspects of modern life causes further alienation and destruction of the human community.

THE UNABOMBER An extreme advocate of the Luddite anti-technology philosophy was the Unabomber. From May 25, 1979, to April 24, 1995, the Unabomber killed three people and injured twenty-three others in sixteen mail bomb incidents. (The nickname Unabomber was derived from "*University-aviation-bomber*" because early bomb victims were people who worked at universities in the field of aviation.) The identity and the exact motives of the Unabomber remained unknown for many years, although authorities strongly sus-pected the culprit was making an anti-technology statement with each of the bombs. Finally, in a letter to the *Washington Post* newspaper in February 1996, the Unabomber offered to stop his siege of terror. In exchange, certain U.S. newspapers agreed to publish the anonymous writer's 35,000-word "Manifesto" against modern technology. Shortly after reading the statement, a man named David Kaczynski came forward and said the Unabomber could be his brother, Theodore Kaczynski. In an intensive investigation the FBI compared wording in Theodore's letters to family members with the writing style in the "Manifesto." Theodore Kaczynski was eventually arrested and charged with the crimes; he pleaded guilty to the charges in 1998. Kaczynski was sentenced to life in solitary confinement, with no possibility of parole, at the "Alcatraz of the Rockies" in Colorado.

Most neo-Luddites seek a return to old methods of commerce and production. They believe that when technology becomes dangerous, alternatives must be found. The new Luddites want to avoid violence and protest. They are willing to settle for a philosophy of conservation and the protection of groups such as the Amish (a religious community that shuns technology). Among the most active neo-Luddite group is the "Do It Yourself" (DIY) movement, which is gaining popularity in Europe and North America. Adopting the motto "Do it yourself, do it right," DIY showrooms, catalogs, and Internet web sites promote various products and projects that support the concept of "self-equity." In a rejection of reliance on technology, self-equity encourages people to create with their own hands and to take an active role in home, family, church, and community.

FOR FURTHER REFERENCE

Books

Sale, Kirkpatrick. *Rebels Against the Future: The Luddites and Their War on the Industrial Revolution—Lessons for the Computer Age.* New York City: Addison Wesley, 1995.

The Southampton Insurrection

AUGUST 21 TO 24, 1831

The Southampton Insurrection was a slave revolt led by Nat Turner, a black slave who lived on a Virginia plantation, in 1831. Although all of the participants in the rebellion were eventually captured and executed, this insurrection marked one of the few times that a large group of slaves banded together to strike out against their white owners. Instead of preparing the way for the abolition of slavery, however, Turner's short-lived and violent rebellion strengthened opposition to freedom for slaves in the South.

Waits to perform special mission

Turner was born in Southampton County, Virginia. His mother was a native African who passed along her intense hatred of slavery to her son. From an early age Turner's mother brought him up to believe that he possessed supernatural powers. Turner learned to read, perhaps from one of his master's sons, and spent his time studying the Bible. He grew to believe that he was an instrument of God, selected to perform a special mission. Turner once said that God communicated to him through voices and through signs in the sky. He eventually became a minister and soon had great influence over the slave community. Many slaves began to call Turner "The Prophet."

Nat Turner's revolt inflamed fears about the dangers of keeping slaves.

Nat Turner, a literate slave and minister, believed that he was chosen by God for a special mission.

Turner was sold twice to other farmers. His last owner was Joseph Travis, who bought the young man shortly before Turner received the inspiration for his rebellion. On August 13, 1831, Turner saw a sign in the sky. This "sign" may have been a solar eclipse (a natural phenomenon in which the light of the Sun is obscured by the Moon passing between the Sun and the Earth). Turner believed this signal meant that the time had come for the slaves to attack their masters. He then shared this message with a handful of trusted followers.

Attacks on white slaveholders

Turner knew that he needed weapons to conduct his war against the slave owners. He planned to lead his band of followers to the Southampton County armory (a storage place for weapons), which was located in the town of Jerusalem, Virginia. After seizing the weapons, the slaves would retreat to a place called Dismal Swamp, where they could hide and defend themselves. Turner hoped that once the rebellion started, other slaves would join the cause. On the night of August 21, Turner and seven fellow slaves began the rebellion by killing Travis and his family. As the group proceeded toward Jerusalem during the following days, nearly seventy other slaves joined the march.

Capture and execution

Turner and his followers killed fifty or sixty whites as they crossed the countryside. In turn, white citizens responded with such overwhelming force that the rebels never reached the armory. Approximately 3,000 state militia (standby military forces) and other armed men surrounded and crushed the rebellion on August 24. Turner's followers were killed immediately or as soon as they were captured. Many other innocent slaves in the area died as a result of the terror the rebellion had caused. Turner somehow escaped capture for six more weeks. When he was found, Turner was tried and then hanged on November 11, 1831.

Controls tightened on slaves

The rebellion that was later referred to as "Nat's Fray" or "Old Nat's War" was doomed from the start. Too few slaves joined Turner in his effort, and he was handicapped by the untrained and unarmed band he did manage to gather. The Southampton Insurrection—especially the violent deaths involved— had a serious impact upon the debate concerning the institution of slavery. Many plantation owners had held on to the notion that slaves were basically contented or simply too passive to rebel. This myth was now destroyed. Fears about the dangers of keeping slaves were greatly inflamed after Turner's revolt.

Throughout the South people called for stricter laws governing slaves' behavior. For example, many people wanted to make teaching a slave to read and write a crime, believing that literacy could lead to knowledge and discontentment. In Virginia the state legislature appointed a committee to make recommendations to the state for the future of slavery. There was intense debate over whether the institution was an essential part of the Southern economy and way of life, or whether it was a dangerous and immoral custom that should be abolished.

Conditions worsen

Ultimately, the Southampton Insurrection led to an even stronger Southern commitment to the institution of slavery. Nat Turner's revolt—although it quickly ended in failure— proved that slaves were capable of organized revolt. This realization resulted in the passage of many new laws restricting the movement, education, and assembly of slaves across the South. (In Virginia, for instance, the legislature decided to preserve the institution of slavery.) Most white Southerners decided it was safer to keep the slavery system in place. In fact, Turner's revolt actually strengthened the Southern defense of its institution.

In the years following the insurrection, Southern blacks continued to escape north using the Underground Railroad (a secret system for helping slaves get to Canada and other "free" regions). In the North, the abolitionist movement gained strength. (Abolitionists worked to outlaw slavery.) In general, conditions for black people who lived in the South did not begin to improve until some time after the Civil War (1861–65).

FOR FURTHER REFERENCE

Books

Goldman, Martin S. *Nat Turner and the Southampton Revolt of 1831*. New York City: F. Watts, 1992.

Oates, Stephen B. *The Fires of Jubilee: Nat Turner's Fierce Rebellion*. New York City: Harper & Row, 1975; reprinted 1990.

John Brown's Raid

OCTOBER 16 TO 18, 1859

In an attempt to obtain weapons for his war against slavery, John Brown (1800–1859) led a handful of men on a raid of the federal armory (a storage place for weapons) at Harpers Ferry, Virginia (now West Virginia). Brown intended to destroy the institution of slavery by launching an attack against Southern slave owners and creating a haven for escaped slaves in the mountains nearby. While Brown's men managed to capture the armory, the group's ultimate goal was never realized. Federal troops overwhelmed Brown's tiny "army" within a few hours. Brown was then put on trial and sentenced to death. The Harpers Ferry raid only served to increase tensions between the North and South; in fact, the Civil War (1861–65) began just seventeen months after Brown's execution.

Plans the impossible

The raid on Harpers Ferry was to be the first step in a master abolitionist plan. (Abolitionists worked to outlaw slavery.) Brown described his idea to a group of black and white abolitionists at a meeting in Chatham, Ontario (a province of Canada) in early 1858. He wanted to create a safe place for escaping slaves in the Allegheny Mountains (a range of mountains running through Pennsylvania, Maryland, West Virginia, and Virginia). He also intended to form an army to liberate slaves from

Radical abolitionist John Brown planned to raid a government arsenal in order to get weapons for an attack against Southern slave owners.

their owners by force. Brown was absolutely committed to bringing the practice of slavery to an end, and he believed radical and violent measures were required to achieve this goal; he also felt that God was on his side in the struggle.

The idea gained strong support—including financial backing—from several well-known abolitionists of the day. Other abolitionists were not so sure about the idea. Some people who sympathized with Brown's aim believed that his methods were misguided. For these people, terrorism and violence were not acceptable, even for such a worthy cause. Others clearly saw that Brown's radical plan was doomed to failure. For example, famous African American abolitionist Frederick Douglass (1817-1895), who met in secret with Brown shortly before the raid, was convinced that Brown's plan would be fatal for escaping slaves—perhaps for "all engaged." After Brown was captured Abraham Lincoln (1809–1865), who would soon be the president of the United States, called the plan "so absurd that [even] the slaves ... saw plainly enough it could not succeed."

Noble purpose, violent methods

The first step in Brown's plan was to take over the armory at the town of Harpers Ferry, Virginia, holding it long enough to seize arms and ammunition. Then he and his band would retreat into the Allegheny Mountains, which, Brown said, God had created in order "that they may one day be a refuge for fugitive slaves." Brown believed that as slaves learned of his actions, more and more of them would rebel against their owners and join his cause. As his guerrilla force gathered strength, it would be able to strike further and further south. (Guerrillas are untrained, mobile groups of soldiers who operate in enemy-held territory.)

With a small band of devoted followers, Brown moved from Kansas to Virginia in the summer of 1859. Posing as a

JOHN BROWN John Brown was born in Torrington, Connecticut, into an abolitionist family. (Abolitionists were people who believed slavery should be outlawed.) Brown's father operated a "station" on the Underground Railroad (a secret system for helping slaves escape north to Canada and other "free" areas). In 1805 the family moved to Hudson, Ohio. In spite of his mother's death when he was eight years old, Brown grew into a strong, self-reliant boy. By the age of ten, he was working alongside his father, farming, hunting, trapping, and making leather from animal skins. Although he never attended school regularly, Brown learned to read by borrowing books from a neighbor. At age sixteen, he decided to become a minister, but an inflammation (infection) of one eye forced him to abandon his studies. He then returned home to help his father in the leather business. Brown later married and became a prosperous businessman.

Brown soon became a local model for enterprising citizens. He was also raising money and seeking hiding places for escaping slaves. Personal tragedy, which struck him repeatedly during the 1830s and 1840s, seemed to fuel Brown's devotion to eliminating slavery. In 1855 Brown and several of his sons moved to Kansas to begin a direct attack on supporters of slavery. Resorting to terrorism to deliver their message, they killed five men in one night as retribution (revenge) for the killing of five abolitionists. Now wanted by the law, Brown successfully freed twelve slaves who were about to be sold and took them north to safety. Brown's master plan was to liberate slaves from the Southern plantations (large farms where slaves worked as laborers). In 1859 Brown and his followers were captured when they raided the federal armory at Harpers Ferry, Virginia. Convinced of the morality of his cause even as he faced death, Brown was hanged on December 2, 1859.

farmer, he rented a house outside Harpers Ferry as a headquarters for his raid. On the evening of October 16, Brown gave the order to proceed to the ferry. His band consisted of sixteen white and five black men. Three recruits stayed at the house to guard supplies, while eighteen men headed out through the cold, rainy night to Harpers Ferry. As they approached the town, the men cut the telegraph wires. Breaking into the armory was not difficult. They took a watchman captive, along with about fifty other people, planning to exchange them later for slaves.

Captured by Robert E. Lee

During the night, several shots were fired, alerting citizens to the trouble. Townspeople took up positions in buildings surrounding the armory. Gunfire was exchanged; the first casual-

An overhead view of Harpers Ferry, Virginia. John Brown's failed raid of the government armory at Harpers Ferry helped to fuel tensions between the North and South over slavery.

ty on Brown's side was a black man named Dangerfield Newby. That evening, Colonel Robert E. Lee (1807–1870), who would later serve as a general for the Confederate army during the Civil War, arrived from Washington, D.C. with a group of U.S. Marines. The troops stormed the fire engine house where Brown's party had retreated. In three minutes, the raiders were overwhelmed. During the fighting, Brown received several saber thrusts to his neck and chest. (A saber is a single-edged sword.) He dropped to the ground, where one of his sons already lay dead and another lay dying.

Faces consequences "like a broken-winged hawk"

Although he was seriously wounded, Brown welcomed the interrogation (formal questioning) that followed because it gave him an audience for his strong convictions regarding slavery. Governor Wise of Virginia, who was present at the interrogation, described the leader of the raid on Harpers Ferry in vivid terms. Brown, he said, was like "a broken-winged hawk, lying on his back, with a fearless eye.... They are mistaken who take Brown to be a madman. He is a bundle of the best nerves I ever saw.... He is a man of clear head, of courage, fortitude, and simple ingenuousness."

Nonetheless, in a matter of days Brown and four members of his band found themselves on trial for treason (the crime of acting to overthrow the government or to impair its functionality). Two Southern lawyers, who were probably not sympathetic to Brown's cause, were appointed to defend the men. Brown was convicted of murder, slave insurrection, and treason against the Commonwealth of Virginia. He was sentenced to be hanged in public on December 2, 1859.

Some 1,500 people were present for Brown's execution. As he stepped up onto the scaffold (an elevated platform for hanging), he spoke these last words: "I, John Brown, am quite certain that the crimes of this guilty land will never be purged away [except] with blood." He was right to assume that bloodshed would follow. The first shots of the Civil War were fired just seventeen months later, marking the beginning of a long and very destructive war. And as they marched, many Northern soldiers remembered the dead abolitionist in song: "John Brown's body lies a-moldering in the grave.... But his soul is marching on."

FOR FURTHER REFERENCE

Books

Everett, Gwen. *John Brown: One Man Against Slavery.* New York City: Rizzoli, 1993.

Scott, John Anthony. *John Brown of Harpers Ferry.* New York City: Facts on File, 1988.

The Triangle Shirtwaist Company Fire

MARCH 25, 1911

The Triangle catastrophe led to a widespread movement for safer working conditions in the United States.

The Triangle Shirtwaist Company fire was one of the worst industrial disasters in American history. On March 25, 1911, 146 Triangle employees—most of them young immigrant women—died while trying to escape a rampaging blaze at the company's sweatshop in New York City. The many victims died because they were trapped in the building and could not be rescued. As the fire swept from the eighth to the ninth and tenth floors, people had to jump from windows because fire truck ladders could only reach between the sixth and seventh floors. Water from fire hoses sprayed only to the seventh floor, and the outside fire escape collapsed in the inferno. The Triangle catastrophe led to a widespread movement for safer working conditions in the United States. Among the results were factory fire codes, child labor laws, and other labor legislation. The Triangle Shirtwaist tragedy also became an historical reference point for people in the early part of the century, much like the assassination of President John F. Kennedy or the crash of the *Challenger* space shuttle have become for us today.

A chance for extra money

The Triangle Shirtwaist Company was a clothing factory owned by Isaac Harris and Max Blanck that produced shirtwaists (women's blouses styled like men's shirts). Widely known as a sweatshop, Triangle employed young women to assemble shirtwaists at low wages for long hours. Most of the women were Italian, Yiddish (Jewish), and German immigrants. The sweatshop was housed in the Asch Building, a steel and concrete fireproofed structure on the corner of Greene Street and Washington Place in lower Manhattan. (Formerly adjacent to the New York University Law School, the building is now part of the New York University campus.) Triangle occupied the eighth, ninth, and tenth floors of the building; other clothing makers were located on the lower floors. On March 25, 1911, a Saturday, shops on the lower floors had closed at noon. That day, however, 850 Triangle workers were putting in overtime to supplement their average weekly earnings of six dollars.

"Fire!"

At 4:45 P.M. the factory bell signaled the end of the work day. Just as employees were getting ready to leave, someone shouted "Fire!" and people began scrambling in an effort to get out of the building. Although the blaze had started on the eighth floor, the message reached the tenth floor first. It came through the teleautograph (a device used for communicating between floors) in the tenth-floor showroom, where workers were pressing the shirtwaists.

The pressers initially dismissed the alarm as a prank, then they smelled smoke. The blaze had started in the eighth-floor cutting room and was feeding on scraps of highly flammable cotton fabric and leaping onto finished garments hanging on racks. Smoke and fire poured upward through the stairways to the ninth floor and toward the tenth. Knowing they could not find any exit routes, the tenth-floor workers scrambled to the roof and called for help. Staff and students at New York University Law School next door lowered a ladder onto the roof, saving almost 150 Triangle employees.

Pandemonium

As these workers fled to safety, however, hundreds of others remained trapped. Out on the street, pedestrians noticed smoke pouring from windows on the eighth floor. Soon the

The burned-out ruins of the Triangle Shirtwaist factory. Over 140 company employees—most of them women—died in the blaze.

observers saw people jumping from windows. By the time fire trucks arrived from Engine Company 72 on Twelfth Street six blocks away, six women lay dead on the pavement. Inside the building on the eighth floor, the foreman and tailors were trying to douse the blaze with fire buckets.

When it became obvious that the fire could not be controlled, 275 women rushed toward the two passenger elevators

Great Misadventures

After the Triangle fire, police transported the bodies of dead workers to the Bellevue Morgue for later identification.

and the single stairway that offered a chance for escape. Since the door to the stairwell opened into the room instead of out toward the hall, however, it immediately slammed shut as the workers pressed against it. Scores of panic-stricken women then tried to crowd into elevator cars that would accommodate only ten people. The two elevator operators made fifteen to twenty trips, each time carrying twelve to fifteen passengers to the street below. In the meantime, someone had managed to open the stairway door. Finally, a number of women were able to flee down the stairs and out onto the street level. The women's clothes had been almost completely burned from their bodies.

Disaster

Pandemonium also reigned on the ninth floor as the fire roared upward and consumed stacks of fabric. Here, women could not even reach the west stairway, which had become a conduit for the smoke and flames. Rushing to the east stairway, they found the door was locked. Then the women tried the fire escape, but the heat forced them back. Finally they ran to the elevator. Once the elevator arrived, it could take only a few people down to street level. At this point, many people sought refuge in a cloakroom and others leaped from windows. In fact, most of the people who attempted to jump to safety came from the ninth floor. After the fire was extinguished, firemen found nineteen bodies melted against the locked stairway door and another twenty-five in the cloakroom.

Fire equipment inadequate

By now thousands of spectators had gathered behind the police barricades. While escape efforts continued, Engine Company 33 rushed to the scene from Great Jones Street. Once the firemen deployed their equipment, they discovered that water from the fire hoses would reach only to the seventh floor and ladders stopped between the sixth and seventh floors. Finally fire fighters were able to gain access to the stairway and began to put out the fire. As they moved from room to room, they found that the building itself had not been damaged. Constructed of steel and concrete, the Asch Building was a fire-proof death trap.

Bodies recovered

Throughout the disaster horse-drawn ambulances lined up on the street. Around 6:00 P.M., about two hours after the fire was detected, ambulances began transporting the dead to

On March 25, 1961, survivors of the Triangle fire gathered in New York City to commemorate the fiftieth anniversary of the tragedy.

Bellevue Morgue about thirty blocks away. At first police requested seventy-five to one hundred coffins, but only sixty-five were available at the morgue. The police had to send a steamboat to Blackwell's Island (now called Franklin D. Roosevelt Island; located in the East River) to pick up 200 coffins.

The slow procession continued throughout the night as relatives and friends of factory workers converged on the morgue to see if their loved ones had died in the tragedy. A final body count revealed that 146 Triangle employees, most of them young women, had been killed by the fire. A few days later a temporary police station was set up to accommodate the people—at first more than 100 a minute—who came to identify the remains.

Labor reforms

An official investigation failed to determine the precise cause of the Triangle Shirtwaist Company fire, but inspectors speculated that a smoker threw a match or a cigarette into a pile of fabric scraps in the eighth-floor cutting room. Harris and Blanck were indicted (required to stand trial) for negligence, on the charge that if doors had not been locked, the victims could have escaped. The men were found innocent, however, on December 28, 1911. Later twenty-three victims' families sued Harris and Blanck. Each family was eventually awarded about seventy-five dollars.

Although the factory owners were not held responsible for the fire, the catastrophe had a lasting impact on labor laws in the United States. In response to public outrage, the New York legislature appointed a commission to investigate sweatshop conditions in New York City. The commission's final report resulted in state laws that provide health, disability, and fire prevention protection to workers. Strict child labor laws were also enacted.

The city of New York created a fire prevention division that became a permanent part of the fire department. Inspectors could enforce codes requiring factories to have doors that opened outward and that remained unlocked during work hours. Companies employing more than twenty-five people above the ground floor had to be equipped with sprinkler systems, and workplaces that had no sprinkler system had to conduct mandatory fire drills. The state legislation and city codes became models for similar measures throughout the country. Another important outcome of the Triangle Shirtwaist tragedy was increased organizational activity by the International Ladies Garment Workers Union (ILGW), which had been formed in 1900.

FOR FURTHER REFERENCE

Books

Kent, Zachary. *The Story of the Triangle Factory Fire*. New York City: Children's Press, 1989.

The Black Sox Baseball Scandal

1919

In 1919 eight members of the Chicago White Sox baseball team conspired to fix the outcome of their World Series games against the Cincinnati Reds. Demoralized by low pay from team owner Charles Comiskey (1859–1931), the players made an arrangement with professional gamblers to lose the series. In return, the players were to receive $100,000. The White Sox lost five games and won three (at that time the World Series consisted of nine games). The deal fell through, however, when the gamblers refused to fulfill their part of the bargain. The fix came to public attention in 1920, and the players' involvement made front-page headlines in newspapers throughout the country. Because of the deal the eight players became known in the media as the "Black Sox." (The rest of the team members were called the "Clean Sox.") The Black Sox were ultimately cleared of criminal charges. Nevertheless, the newly appointed baseball commissioner, Kenesaw Mountain Landis, had the players' names and statistics (hits and runs averages) removed from major league record books. He also banned the men from the sport for life.

Even though they were acquitted of all criminal charges, the "Black Sox" were banned from baseball for life.

The national pastime

The Black Sox scandal created a sensation because baseball occupies a special place in the hearts of Americans. For more

The Chicago White Sox baseball team in 1919. Several team members—later referred to as the "Black Sox"—were involved in a plot to throw the World Series.

than 100 years the game has been called the favorite national pastime. Many baseball fans regard the players as heroes, and depend on the teams to compete with honesty, fairness, and skill. The highlight of the baseball season is the World Series, a succession of games in which two teams try to win the world championship. The two competitors are the teams with the best season record (or most games won) from the National League and the American League. In the 1919 World Series the Cincinnati Reds of the National League were meeting the Chicago White Sox of the American League. Since the Chicago team had the better players, they were expected to win the championship.

Talented players

The eight players involved in the Black Sox scandal were Eddie Cicotte, Claude "Lefty" Williams, Charles "Chick" Gandil, Charles "Swede" Risberg, George "Buck" Weaver, Joe "Shoeless Joe" Jackson, Oscar "Happy" Felsch, and Fred

McMullin. The idea to fix the 1919 World Series originated with Gandil, the first baseman who had connections to professional gamblers. Joining Gandil as a ringleader in the plot was Risberg, a shortstop (the player positioned between second and third bases) who had a quick temper.

The success of the fix was in the hands of starting pitchers Cicotte and Williams. Potentially one of baseball's greatest pitchers, Cicotte was known for his ability to throw a ball with precision control. In 1917 he had won 28 games and earned a 1.53 ERA (earned run average; the number of earned runs scored by base hits against him in a nine-inning game). Outfielder Jackson was an equally outstanding player. In fact, next to Ty Cobb (1886-1961), he was the best player of the era. Jackson still holds the third-highest batting average (.356) in the history of baseball. Jackson was given the nickname of "Shoeless" after he played in a minor league (the league in which players train for the major league) game in his socks because a new pair of shoes hurt his feet. Felsch was known for his fielding and throwing ability, and he had a lifetime batting average of .293. Third baseman Weaver, who had a career batting average of .333, did not participate in the fix—but he knew about it.

Fix revealed

By 1919 major league baseball had a serious problem with players fixing games. The best-known case involved Hal Chase, a first baseman for the Cincinnati Reds and then the New York Giants. Chase had tried repeatedly to recruit pitchers to lose games. Team owners and the league president, however, took steps to stop Chase's activities so the image of the sport would not be tarnished. In 1919, John McGraw (1873–1934), manager of the New York Giants, removed Chase from the lineup and he never played another game.

Baseball officials were therefore confident that, by stopping Chase, they had eliminated any chance of players fixing games. These hopes were dashed in 1920 when a Cook County grand jury in Chicago, Illinois, began an investigation into baseball gambling. In the course of testimony, witness Rube Benton, a pitcher for the New York Giants, said he had learned from Chase that the 1919 World Series had been fixed. Benton testified that Chase had won $40,000 in bets on the games. Furthermore, Benton claimed to have seen a telegram from a man named Sleepy Bill Burns that proved Burns had worked on behalf of gamblers in the World Series deal.

Deal falls apart

More evidence came from a front-page story in a Philadelphia newspaper on September 27, 1920. A gambler named Bill Maharg told the reporter that several White Sox players had taken bribes to lose the first two games of the series. According to Maharg, White Sox pitcher Cicotte met Burns and Maharg in New York City. Cicotte reportedly said the team would lose the series for $100,000, which had to be paid before the series started. To finance the deal Maharg and Burns tried to recruit Philadelphia gamblers. They were not interested, but suggested approaching a well-known New York gambler named Arnold Rothstein.

At first Rothstein showed little enthusiasm, then he decided to fund the scheme. The go-between would be Rothstein's bodyguard, Abe Attell, a former featherweight boxing champion. Maharg said the arrangement turned sour right away because Attell would not turn over the $100,000 to the players. Attell said he needed the money for betting, but he finally agreed to a compromise by offering $20,000 for each lost game. When the White Sox were defeated in the first game, Attell would still not pay. After the second loss, he parted with just $10,000, which was given to Cicotte. By now the players were angry with the gamblers, so they decided to win game three. When the White Sox won, the gamblers believed they had been double-crossed, so they would not deliver any money.

Players indicted

After the World Series, all of the guilty players were re-signed by Comiskey for the 1920 baseball season. He had even doubled some of their salaries. Then reports of the fix appeared in the newspapers in early 1921. Finally the players were forced to come forward and testify before the grand jury. Cicotte and Jackson were the first to confess. Cicotte described how he had purposely lost the first and fourth games by not throwing at full speed, making a wild throw, and using other tactics. He said he received the $10,000, which he used to help pay off the mortgage on his farm. Jackson admitted to fielding and throwing inadequately and striking out once when White Sox runners were on base and possibly could have scored. When Jackson was leaving the courthouse after his testimony one day, a small boy supposedly said to him: "Say it ain't so, Joe!"—a plea that today is still a reminder of the Black Sox scandal.

As Cicotte and Jackson continued their testimony, they implicated the six other players. Seven of the eight men—now called the Black Sox—were indicted (ordered to stand trial) by the grand jury. (Charges against McMullin were dropped for lack of evidence.) Comiskey had to suspend the players, but he promised they would be reinstated on the team if they were proved innocent. The players then met with Comiskey's attorneys. As Williams began discussing his role in the scheme, the plot became even more complex. He identified two other gamblers, Nat Evans and Sport Sullivan, who offered to pay $10,000 to eight players. Williams would receive $10,000 for losing the second game. After talking with Evans and Sullivan, Williams learned about the deal with Burns and Attell. In spite of all the promises, though, Williams received only $5,000 when he lost the fourth game. Years later Williams's wife revealed that the gamblers threatened to kill her if he did not lose the eighth game. The White Sox lost.

Trial begins

The seven Black Sox and ten gamblers were arraigned (called to stand trial) in February 1921. Before the trial started, Robert Crowe, the district attorney, was informed that the judge had ruled the indictments were faulty. Crowe asked for a postponement of the trial because crucial records of the grand jury hearings were missing from his files. The judge denied the request. The trial opened on June 27, 1921. The seven players showed up, but the gamblers were less cooperative. Many said they were too sick to appear, but Attell was the most ingenious in avoiding prosecution. He said he was not the Attell who had been indicted, and he produced witnesses to prove his claim.

Case disintegrates

The case against the Black Sox disintegrated when the prosecuting attorney repeated Crowe's report that important evidence was missing from the files. The documents were the original confessions of the players and their waivers of immunity. It was later learned that two former prosecutors had stolen the evidence before they left office. Their purpose was to make sure there was no way to incriminate Rothstein. Lawyers for Rothstein and Comiskey were behind the deception. The lack of original documents muddied the case, although the trial judge said unsigned carbon copies were admissible.

Before the jury deliberated, the judge ruled that there was not enough evidence against players Weaver and Felsch and a gambler named Carl Zork. He set these men free. The jury took only a few hours to reach a decision to acquit (find not guilty) another gambler and the remaining players. (The cases against the other gamblers were either settled out of court or dismissed.) Chaos broke out in the courtroom. The jurors, who were clearly White Sox fans, carried the jubilant players around on their shoulders. Then players and jurors gathered at a nearby restaurant to continue the celebration.

Black Sox banned

The Black Sox hoped that since they had been acquitted, they could start playing baseball again. The newly appointed baseball commissioner, Kenesaw Mountain Landis, shocked the sports world by banning all of the Black Sox—including McMullin—from the sport for life. Weaver, who did not participate in the fix, repeatedly petitioned Landis for reinstatement, but the commissioner would not budge. He said Weaver had "guilty knowledge" of the deception, so he shared responsibility for the World Series fix with the other players.

In the aftermath of the Black Sox scandal, it was nearly impossible to sort out precisely what happened. It is true a plot existed, and the players initiated contact with gamblers for the purposes of fixing the games. Yet no one knows exactly how much money was involved or which players were paid off. The Black Sox lacked a specific plan for throwing the games, and they even contradicted each other about the games that had been fixed. There is no way to be certain which games the

Cincinnati Reds actually won on their own because the White Sox were a superior team.

Hurt by the legal system

The Black Sox were ill-served by the legal system. They confessed their guilt and waived (gave up) their rights without a lawyer present. In the case of Jackson, who was illiterate (he could not read or write), a confession may have been given for the benefit of the gamblers. The Clean Sox also knew something was amiss, but they did not alert Comiskey or law enforcement officials.

At first the Black Sox tried to reestablish their careers by joining semiprofessional "outlaw" clubs. But Landis would not tolerate a violation of his ban, and he threatened to blacklist (prevent from playing) any player who participated in a game with an ineligible player. Some of the Black Sox continued their careers under aliases (assumed names) in obscure leagues, thereby defying Landis. Their lives, however, were never the same again. The 1919 Black Sox scandal was later explored in *Eight Men Out* (1988), a film by writer-director John Sayles (who appears as newspaperman Ring Lardner). Based on a book by Eliot Asinof, the movie gives a factual account of the Black Sox players' deal with the gamblers.

FOR FURTHER REFERENCE

Books

Gropman, Donald. *Say It Ain't So, Joe!* New York City: Little, Brown, 1979.

The Dionne Quintuplets

BORN IN 1934

"Quintland" became a huge tourist attraction, bringing in as many as 10,000 visitors a month.

T he Dionne quintuplets were born on May 28, 1934, in Toronto, Canada. The first quintuplets known to have survived infancy, the babies weighed between one pound, eight ounces and two and a half pounds at birth. Their survival was considered a miracle (a sixth sibling had been aborted during the third month of pregnancy). Previously, multiple-birth infants had lived only a few days. Even more remarkably, the Dionnes—Annette, Cecile, Emilie, Marie, and Yvonne—were identical. The girls caused an immediate media sensation. It seemed that the public had an insatiable need to follow even the most minute details of their development. The babies were dubbed "the quints" and soon they and their attending physician, Dr. Allan Roy Dafoe, became international celebrities.

The quints were also the subjects of intense scientific research. Doctors determined that a primary reason for the Dionnes' survival after a premature birth was that the Hospital for Sick Children in Toronto had provided mother's milk and incubators for the babies' care. Researchers at the University of Toronto further learned that the quints originated from a single fertilized egg that had repeatedly duplicated and produced six embryos. Consequently, the Dionne babies all had identical genetic material. Scientific discovery was quickly overshad-

The Dionne quintuplets and their attending physician, Dr. Allan Roy Dafoe. Dafoe and the Dionne family priest convinced Oliva and Elzire Dionne to exhibit their children in an effort to raise money.

owed, however, by the controversy over who would raise the quints. Eventually the government of Ontario intervened and made the children wards of the state. Thus began a misadventure that permanently scarred the Dionne quintuplets' lives.

Government steps in

The parents of Annette, Cecile, Emilie, Marie, and Yvonne Dionne were extremely poor. Oliva and Elzire Dionne were French-Canadian farmers who could not afford to support their five newborn babies (the couple already had five children; four others were born after the quints). In an effort to raise money, Oliva Dionne sold the rights to exhibit the quints to promoter Ivan Spear. He had been urged to take this unusual step by Dafoe, the physician who delivered the quints, and Father

Daniel Routhier, the Dionne family priest. Spear promised Dionne a twenty-three percent return on admission fees.

Once the deal was made public, however, outraged citizens protested the commercialization of the babies. The Ontario government then stepped in and took the quints away from their parents. The infants were made wards (placed under the protection) of the state, under the supervision of Dafoe. Next the government created a board of guardians that would oversee the girls' care. Oliva and Elzire Dionne were not appointed to the board because they were considered to be ignorant and barely competent.

"Quintland" a tourist attraction

Instead of giving the quints a normal life out of public view, the government put them on display—ironically, just as their parents planned to do with Spear. The province of Ontario built a house on the Dionne farm, across the road from the family home, near Corbeil, Ontario. Large, one-way mirrors were installed so that curiosity seekers could observe the children from a horseshoe-shaped observatory outside. Nicknamed "Quintland," the nine-room nursery became a huge tourist attraction, bringing as many as 10,000 visitors a month. The income was phenomenal. The Dionne attraction saved nearby Callander from possible bankruptcy, and it was a boon to the economy of North Bay. A forerunner to today's theme parks, Quintland eventually made $500 million. In 1941 a $1 million trust fund was established for the girls from the Quintland profits and the sale of memorabilia and souvenirs.

With the assistance of the government, the quints were involved in other money-making endeavors. They made three Hollywood movies: The Country Doctor (1936), Reunion (1936), and Five of a Kind (1938). They endorsed hundreds of products, including Carnation Milk, Remington typewriters, corn syrup, and Quaker Oats. Quint dolls outsold the Shirley Temple doll. (Shirley Temple was a popular child film star during the 1930s.)

The commercial potential of the Dionnes was utilized to the fullest extent. The girls were used to sell war bonds and their pictures appeared on pencils. Although the government had claimed it could raise the girls better than their parents, it

EXPLOITATION AND GREED

At the time of the Dionne quintuplets' birth during the Great Depression (1929–39; a period of severe economic hardship), the children were greeted as a ray of sunshine. Millions of people around the world were curious about these tiny babies, who had defied great odds in order to stay alive. But the quints' childhood was controlled first by the Ontario government and then by their own parents. The five girls became victims of greed and exploitation. The surviving Dionnes were not able to overcome this mistreatment. Alienated from their sisters and brothers—who viewed them as money hungry—the Dionnes began a campaign in the 1990s to regain some of the money they believe was taken from them. Long after the public fascination with them had died, the Dionne quintuplets were left embittered and angry.

is clear the Dionnes were exploited commercially. The children were kept on exhibit until they were nine years old. Then in 1943, after a nine-year legal battle, Oliva and Elzire Dionne regained custody of their five daughters. The little girls' fishbowl existence was brought to an end. The reunion was not a happy one, however, because the quints never fit in with their nine brothers and sisters. They grew to feel that the rest of the family blamed them for their hardship and misery.

Unhappy adult lives

At the age of eighteen the quints left home and moved together to Montreal, Quebec, where they initially shared an apartment. They started lives independent of their family, and managed to remain anonymous as adults. When they were twenty-one the quints received the first of three installments on two-thirds of $800,000 from the trust fund (one-third was set aside for the quints' children; the final installment was paid in 1979). Despite this money, the girls could never quite escape the memories of their childhood and the conflict they experienced when they were reunited with their family.

During the early years in Montreal, Marie opened a flower shop and Yvonne and Cecile worked as nurses. All of the Dionnes, except for Yvonne, got married; among them, the quints had ten children. Each marriage, however, ended unhappily in a costly divorce settlement. Two of the quints died. Emilie suffocated to death after an epileptic seizure at age twenty. Fifteen years later, in 1969, Marie died from a blood clot in the brain. Her life had been particularly unhappy. She became an alcoholic and suffered a deep depression after separating from her husband. Three days after her death, she was found in her Montreal apartment. The surviving quints returned to Corbeil only twice, for their parents' funerals in 1979 and 1986.

Publish autobiographies

In 1965, before Marie's death, Marie, Cecile, Annette, and Yvonne published their first autobiography, *We are Five: The Dionne Quintuplets.* In the book the women accused their father of squandering $200,000. Thirty years later the three surviving quints, Cecile, Annette, and Yvonne, hired Jean-Yves Soucy to ghostwrite an updated biography, *The Dionne Quints: Family Secrets* (1995). The new book was even more accusatory. The Dionne sisters said they were breaking their long silence to reveal that their father, who died in 1979, had sexually abused them. They claimed the abuse began when they were reunited with their parents in 1943. At the time Annette approached the priest at their private school. He simply replied that she and her sisters should love their parents, and it was their responsibility to protect themselves against their father. After the book was published, one of their sisters denied the charges, saying the surviving quints were motivated by greed.

File lawsuit

The Dionnes also renewed their claims that the money made from Quintland and the sale of promotional products had been squandered or otherwise misused. For instance, they reported that approximately $50,000 was spent to build a new home for their reunited family in 1943. The quints questioned why they received only $800,000 from a trust fund that supposedly contained $1 million. Cecile charged that the trust-fund contract was flawed by not taking inflation into consideration. Bertrand Dionne Langlois, the son of Cecile, was especially critical of how the Dionne money was spent. He stated that a large portion of the funds went to pay guardian fees, Quintland staff salaries, and operating costs. He noted that the observatory outside Quintland cost $200,000 to build, and the construction bill for a public toilet was $5,000.

Considering the amount of money brought in by Quintland, the Dionnes should have been set for life. Since the trust fund had been exhausted long ago, however, the quints filed a $10 million suit against the Ontario government. (They said they needed an income for their old age.) While waiting for the settlement of the suit, the Dionnes received a sizable consulting fee for *Million Dollar Babies,* a television movie shown on the Canadian Broadcasting Company (CBC-TV) and the Columbia Broadcasting System (CBS-TV) in 1995. In 1998, Yvonne, Cecile, and Annette were finally awarded $4 million in compensation from the Ontario government.

FOR FURTHER REFERENCE

Periodicals

Came, Barry. "A Family Tragedy." *Maclean's.* November 21, 1994.

Nicholls, Jane. "Life with Father: Three Remaining Quints Accuse Oliva Dionne of Sexual Abuse." *People Weekly.* October 16, 1995, pp. 176–77.

The *War of the Worlds* Broadcast

OCTOBER 31, 1938

On Halloween night, October 31, 1938, *Mercury Theatre on the Air* broadcast a radio adaptation of *The War of the Worlds,* a novel by H. G. Wells. Presented as a news report, the program depicted a Martian invasion of the United States. During the broadcast, mass panic erupted among listeners who believed the end of the world was at hand. At the center of the panic was twenty-three-year-old Orson Welles (1915–1985), the founder of the Mercury Theatre and the lead actor in the broadcast. Welles and his associates had no intention of pulling off a daring hoax, thinking the broadcast would be no more than an entertaining story for Halloween night. Six million Americans listened to the *Mercury Theatre* show, which previously had broadcast adaptations of such books as Charles Dickens's *Oliver Twist* and Charlotte Brontë's *Jane Eyre.* One million listeners, however, believed they were hearing reports of an actual invasion. This huge misunderstanding pointed out the gullibility of the American public. Welles, on the other hand, emerged as a boy wonder and genius of American theater and screen.

One million radio listeners thought they were hearing an actual Martian invasion of the United States.

Striving for realism

The radio script for *The War of the Worlds* was adapted from the Wells novel by Howard Koch for live broadcast on the

Columbia Broadcasting System (CBS) radio network. When Welles first saw the script, he called it "silly" and demanded more realistic details. (Ironically, Welles would later try to claim authorship of the radio play after the broadcast had achieved notoriety.) The CBS legal department, however, would not allow the names of real organizations to be used; it would only approve the use of place names. Finally, it was decided that realism would be heightened by interrupting the program with news bulletins and by using authentic sounds effects. For instance, actor Frank Readick repeatedly listened to a recording of the broadcast of the *Hindenburg* crash (see "Science and Technology" entry) so he could duplicate the increasing desperation of the reporter who described the explosion.

On the air live

As soon as *The War of the Worlds* was on the air, Mercury Theatre announced that the broadcast was fiction, not reality. In fact, four times during the show this announcement was made: "You are listening to a CBS presentation of Orson Welles and the *Mercury Theatre on the Air* in an original dramatization of *The War of the Worlds* by H.G. Wells." Yet right away, the show seemed extremely real. One reason was the high level of the performances. Welles, a fine actor, played the lead role of Professor Pierson at the Princeton University observatory, a scientist who was studying the invasion.

Another reason was that many people in the radio audience (over twelve percent) had just switched stations from the *Edgar Bergen and Charlie McCarthy Show* (a popular program starring a ventriloquist and his smart-mouthed dummy) to *Mercury Theatre on the Air*. These new listeners had not heard the initial warning. Instead, they heard an ominous description of carnage caused by Martians.

The broadcast begins

The story unfolds as a reporter (actor Readick) describes the invaders from his post at Grover's Mill, New Jersey, where the spaceship has landed. The Martians appear as frightening, saliva-dripping monsters with dead, snake-like eyes. The sense

◄ Orson Welles acts out the role of Professor Pierson during his famous 1938 broadcast of H. G. Wells's *War of the Worlds*.

of doom in the hour-long show escalates as the Martians, using ray-guns, incinerate all humans within their sight. The Martians quickly conquer the East Coast of the United States, including New York City, for there is no defense against their powerful machines. Professor Pierson (actor Welles) follows the invaders to Central Park, where he discovers they have been conquered by a flock of blackbirds. Welles concluded the broadcast by announcing: "That grinning, glowing, globular invader of your living room is an inhabitant of the pumpkin patch, and if your doorbell rings and nobody's there, that was no Martian ... it's Hallowe'en." The show's finale made clear that the fictional Martians had been defeated. This point, however, was missed by many listeners.

Audience tricked themselves

Even before the show was over, people called CBS to confirm that the invasion was real. As one listener said, "I just naturally thought it was real. Why shouldn't I?" After the show ended, CBS continued to broadcast bulletins announcing that there had been no invasion. But finding out the show was a radio play did not satisfy those people who had fooled themselves—they became angry. Now seeing the broadcast as a cruel hoax, some of the audience made threats of reprisal against CBS and Orson Welles. Others sought legal remedies through the courts, but all the lawsuits were unsuccessful. Critics cried for censorship, but they were shouted down by the free press.

Welles was shaken, even apologetic, about the misadventure that resulted from his broadcast of *The War of the Worlds*. After reflecting the listeners' panic, however, he once told an interviewer: "Under the old system the child felt at home among ghosts and goblins, and did not grow up to be a pushover for sensational canards [false reports]. But the ban on gruesome fairy tales, terrifying nursemaids and other standard sources of horror has left most of the population without any protection against fee-fi-fo-fum stuff."

Princeton professor studies mass hysteria

In 1940, two years after *The War of the Worlds* broadcast, Princeton University social psychologist Hadley Cantrill conducted a study of the panic. In his book, *Invasion from Mars*, Cantrill concluded the major reason was radio, a mass medium that formed "the largest grouping of people ever known" at the time. According to Cantrill, it "is estimated that of the 32,000,000 families in the United States, 27,500,000 have radios—a greater proportion than have telephones, automobiles, plumbing, electricity, newspapers or magazines." Therefore, the potential for mass hysteria was heightened significantly.

Cantrill went on to describe how people reacted to the show: "Long before the broadcast had ended, people all over the United States were praying, crying, fleeing frantically to escape death from the Martians. Some ran to rescue loved ones. Others telephoned farewells or warnings, hurried to inform neighbors, sought information from newspapers or radio stations, summoned ambulances and police cars." Cantrill's study captured the depth of confusion and the extent of the social disarray caused by a radio show that was intended simply as Halloween entertainment.

FOR FURTHER REFERENCE

Books

Wells, H. G. *The War of the Worlds*. New York City: Random House, 1991.

The McCarthy Communist Scare

1950 TO 1954

Senator Joseph R. McCarthy brought about his own downfall during the nationally televised Army-McCarthy hearings in 1954.

On February 9, 1950, Senator Joseph R. McCarthy of Wisconsin addressed the Ohio County Women's Republican Club in Wheeling, West Virginia. During his speech McCarthy made the astounding revelation that the U.S. State Department had been infiltrated by Communists: "While I cannot take the time to name all of the men in the State Department who have been named as members of the Communist Party and members of a spy ring," McCarthy said, "I have here in my hand a list of two hundred and five [people] that were known to the Secretary of State as being members of the Communist Party and who nevertheless are still working and shaping the policy of the State Department." (McCarthy later revised his figure downward to eighty-one and then to fifty-seven.)

McCarthy's charges eventually led to a senatorial investigation. Although the senators concluded that McCarthy had perpetrated a "fraud and a hoax," he continued to wage a ruthless anti-communist campaign for four years. In the process McCarthy ruined lives and careers. He brought about his own downfall, however, in the nationally televised Army-McCarthy hearings in 1954. Afterward the hearings, the U.S. Senate censured the senator for his outrageous behavior. The form of persecution and social conformity promoted by McCarthy and his aides gave rise to the term "McCarthyism."

Communism in the United States

At the time McCarthy made his charges against the State Department, the United States was gripped by fears of a communist takeover of the government. (Communist doctrine advocates a totalitarian system of government in which a single authoritarian party has political control. Under this system there is no private property and the state controls manufacturing and industry.) America's greatest communist enemy was the Union of Soviet Socialist Republics (USSR; also referred to as the Soviet Union). Communists had been active in the United States since the 1930s, when the Communist Party had attracted people who opposed fascism. (Fascism is a political philosophy that exalts nation and race over individuals.) By 1939 Communists were working in the government, had joined the labor movement, and were active in certain intellectual circles. They were also prominent in "popular front" organizations (leftist political parties), and communist cells (small political units) that operated in Washington, D.C.

The Communist Party in the United States lost its appeal as an anti-fascist force, however, after the communist purge trials and executions in the Soviet Union that lasted from 1936 to 1938. Many American Communists became further disillusioned after the signing of the Soviet-German nonaggression pact in 1939. (Under the terms of this treaty the USSR agreed not to invade Germany, which was headed by the Nazi government of Adolf Hitler [1889–1945].)

Conflict arose, however, when the Soviet Union became America's ally during World War II (1939–45). As the war drew to a close, U.S. officials learned that Communists had been engaged in subversion (a systematic attempt to overthrow the government) and espionage (spying). In 1945 federal authorities raided the offices of *Amerasia,* a Communist-sponsored monthly journal on Far Eastern affairs. The officials found many secret U.S. diplomatic and military documents. Meanwhile, a Canadian royal commission revealed that several Russian spy rings had operated in Canada during the war, and that a leading scientist had sent atomic secrets to Russia.

Hiss tried as spy

State Department employee Alger Hiss was accused of passing top-secret documents to the Russian government.

In response to these and other revelations, on March 22, 1947, President Harry S Truman (1884–1972) ordered a four-year investigation into the loyalty of all federal employees. Public concern about communism continued to grow, especially as additional evidence of disloyalty was disclosed. The most significant case involved Alger Hiss (born in 1904), a lawyer who had held various posts in the U.S. State Department, including coordinator of American foreign policy conferences. In 1947 Hiss left government service to become president of the Carnegie Endowment for International Peace. The following year Whittaker Chambers (1901–1961), a magazine editor and former Communist Party member, claimed that Hiss had smuggled top-secret State Department documents to the Russians.

Among those people who demanded an investigation of Hiss was California congressman Richard M. Nixon (1913–1996), a member of the House Un-American Activities Committee. (As president of the United States, Nixon was involved in the Watergate scandal in 1974 and became the only president to resign from office [see "Society" entry].) Although Hiss denied all charges, he was indicted on two counts of perjury (lying to the court). At the end of Hiss's 1949 trial, the jury was unable to reach a verdict. A year later Hiss was found guilty in a second trial and sentenced to five years in prison.

The Hiss case caused considerable public debate. Hiss supporters contended that the Federal Bureau of Investigation (FBI) had tampered with evidence to gain a conviction. After being released from prison a year early in 1954 for good behavior, Hiss continued to maintain his innocence.

"Red scare" reaches height

During the Hiss case, other disquieting events occurred. In September 1949, President Truman announced that the Rus-

HOUSE UN-AMERICAN ACTIVITIES COMMITTEE A forerunner to Joseph McCarthy's campaign to identify Communists in government was the House Un-American Activities Committee (HUAC). Formed in 1938 to investigate disloyalty and subversive organizations, the HUAC later focused on finding Communists in government. The committee used many of the same tactics for which McCarthy became infamous, including pressuring witnesses, making reckless accusations, and presuming people were guilty without proof.

HUAC is perhaps best known for its 1947 investigation of the entertainment industry. Performers, writers, directors, producers, and technicians were called before the committee and asked if they "were now or ever had been" members of the Communist Party. People who refused to answer were cited for contempt of Congress and then "blacklisted" by the entertainment industry. Not only did these people lose their jobs, but most were unable to find work anywhere for years to come. A group of especially uncooperative witnesses, called the Hollywood Ten, were actually sent to prison. HUAC was renamed the House Internal Security Committee in 1969 and finally abolished in 1975. In 1976 film maker Woody Allen wrote, directed, and starred in *The Front*, a comedy-satire about blacklisted writers and performers in the 1950s.

sians had exploded an atomic bomb. That same year, the anti-communist Chinese leader Chiang Kai-shek (1887–1975) and his Nationalist government were overthrown by a Communist regime and forced to flee to Formosa (now Taiwan), an island off the coast of China. Many Americans demanded an explanation for these events. The popular feeling was that Communists working within the U.S. government had not only sold out the Nationalists to the Chinese Communists, but had also given atomic secrets to the Russians. These suspicions seemed to be justified in 1950, when the British arrested an atomic scientist named Klaus Fuchs (1912–1988) for transmitting secret information to the Russians from 1943 to 1947. Fuchs pleaded guilty and was sent to prison.

McCarthy capitalizes on fear

In 1950 McCarthy was searching for a political issue, and he found one in the "red scare." When he proclaimed to the women's club in West Virginia that "card-carrying Communists" were working in the State Department, he caused a panic. Immediately McCarthy found himself in the media spot-

In 1950 Wisconsin senator Joseph McCarthy claimed that Communist spies were working in the U.S. State Department.

light. The Senate Committee on Foreign Relations headed by Millard Tydings (1890–1961), a Democratic Senator from Maryland, called a hearing to investigate McCarthy's charges. During testimony before the committee, McCarthy was unable to name 205, or 81, or even 57 Communists in the State Department (or any other government agency).

Rebuking McCarthy for making unsubstantiated and distorted claims, the Tydings Committee concluded that he had perpetrated a fraud and a hoax on the Senate and the American people. The committee members charged that McCarthy's statements represented "perhaps the most nefarious campaign of half-truths and untruths in the history of the Republic." McCarthy's supporters nonetheless hailed him as a patriot and defender of American values. Critics accused him of engaging in a witch-hunt and violating civil liberties, but their voices were drowned out in the public obsession with spies and rumors of spies.

McCarthy ruins lives

Now a media star, McCarthy simply shifted his attack from the State Department to diplomats and other officials who worked with foreign countries. One such person was Owen Lattimore, director of the Page School of International Relations at Johns Hopkins University, whom McCarthy called "the top espionage agent" in America. Although Lattimore was tried on charges of spying, he was found innocent in 1952. That same year McCarthy became chair of both the Government Committee on Operations of the Senate and the permanent subcommittee on investigations. This position gave him the power he needed to seize government documents and target spies. McCarthy intensified his assault, giving addresses on radio and appearing on television. He accused Republicans and Democrats alike of being Communist "sympathizers."

Many Republicans were happy with McCarthy's newfound political clout; in fact, some analysts believe that this power helped get a Republican candidate—Dwight D. Eisenhower (1890–1969)—elected president in 1952. (Interestingly, at one point McCarthy even questioned the new president's loyalty.) After the Republicans had taken control of Congress in 1953, however, certain party members began speaking out against McCarthy. Among them was Senator Margaret Chase Smith of Maine (1897–1995), who said she was not proud of the Senate being used for "selfish political gain at the sacrifice of individual reputations and national unity." Yet McCarthy continued his crusade to track down Communists in widely publicized hearings. During these hearings he made undocumented charges and flung reckless accusations. In the process he ruined careers and brought shame upon innocent people.

McCarthy self-destructs

McCarthy's power trip came to an end in 1954. In April McCarthy accused Secretary of the Army Robert T. Stevens and his staff of concealing evidence of espionage at Fort Monmouth, New Jersey, information that McCarthy's committee was seeking. The army responded by charging McCarthy and one of his aides with improperly pressuring an army private at Fort Monmouth for information. Later that spring, the Army-McCarthy hearings were held on national television.

JOSEPH R. MCCARTHY Joseph R. McCarthy (1908–1957) was born near Appleton, Wisconsin. He began his career as an attorney, then served as a circuit judge (a judge who has jurisdiction over several districts) from 1940 to 1942. During World War II (1939–45) he enlisted in the marines. After the war, in 1946, McCarthy was elected to the U.S. Senate. Upon his re-election in 1952, he was named chair of both the Government Committee on Operations and the permanent subcommittee on investigations.

During his first four years in office, McCarthy had a relatively undistinguished record. In 1950, however, he electrified the nation with charges that "card-carrying Communists" had infiltrated the U.S. State Department. Testifying before the Senate Committee on Foreign Relations, McCarthy exploited public fears of communism. *Point of Order,* a film about McCarthy's anticommunism campaign, was released in 1964. A videocassette version is available under the title *Death of a Witch Hunter* (1986).

During the thirty-six day hearings, an estimated twenty million people watched as McCarthy responded to the accusations. In August he and his staff were cleared of the army's charges, but by this time public sentiment had turned against the senator. Then, on December 22, 1954, the Senate censured McCarthy for bringing the Senate "into dishonor and disrepute" and thus impairing its "dignity." Although McCarthy completed his term in the Senate (1956), his influence waned as a result of his outrageous behavior. He died a defeated and broken man in 1957.

FOR FURTHER REFERENCE

Books

Belfrage, Cedric. *The American Inquisition, 1945–1960: A Profile of the "McCarthy Era."* New York City: Thunder's Mouth Press, 1989.

The Rosenberg Case

JUNE 15, 1950 TO JUNE 19, 1953

O n June 19, 1953, Julius and Ethel Rosenberg became the first U.S. citizens to be executed for espionage (spying). In a controversial trial that attracted international attention, the couple were convicted of heading a Communist spy ring that passed top-secret U.S. military information to the Soviet Union. The Rosenberg trial was one of the most sensational events of the mid-twentieth century. Many people were critical of the government's case against the couple. These critics claimed that the intensely anti-communist climate in the United States during the 1950s led to an exaggeration of circumstantial evidence against the Rosenbergs, who were members of the Communist Party. Legal experts still contend that the information Julius Rosenberg obtained while working for the U.S. Army was of little value; they also believe that the couple's death sentence was too harsh.

Many legal experts believe that the Rosenbergs were victims of a "witch-hunt."

Communism in the United States

During the 1930s, communism became a strong force in the United States, particularly among people who opposed fascism. (Fascism is a political philosophy that exalts nation and race over individuals.) By 1939 Communists were working in the American government, had joined the labor movement, and were active in certain intellectual circles. The Communist

Julius and Ethel Rosenberg were the first American citizens executed for spying against their government. Many legal experts are still questioning the fairness of the couple's trial and sentence.

Party in the United States lost its appeal as an anti-fascist force, however, after the communist purge trials and executions in the Union of Soviet Socialist Republics (USSR; also referred to as the Soviet Union) from 1936 to 1938. Many American Communists became further disillusioned after the signing of the Soviet-German non-aggression pact in 1939. (Under the terms of this treaty the USSR agreed not to invade Germany, which was headed by the Nazi government of Adolf Hitler [1889–1945].)

Conflicts arose, however, when the Soviet Union became a member of the Allied forces during World War II (1939–45. The Allied forces—which included Britain, Canada, France, and the United States—fought the Axis powers. The Axis group included Germany, Italy, and Japan.) As the war drew to a close, U.S. officials learned that Communists had been engaged in subversion (a systematic attempt to overthrow the government) and espionage. In the 1950s, Americans began to fear a communist takeover of the U.S. government, and anti-communist hysteria spread throughout the country.

The Rosenbergs and the Soviet spy network

The generally accepted version of the Rosenberg story begins with a network of Communist spies who were working in the United States, Britain, and other Western countries during World War II. One important infiltrator was Klaus Fuchs (1912–1988), a German-born British physicist and Communist spy. From 1940 to 1941 Fuchs was interned (held in custody) in Canada as an enemy alien. (An enemy alien is a citizen of an enemy country. Fuchs was a native of Germany, which at the time was at war with the Allied forces.) In 1943 Fuchs went to work on the development of the atomic bomb in the United States. Even before he arrived, however, Fuchs had become deeply involved in spying for the Soviet Union. He was in regular contact with Semion Kremer, the secretary of the

Russian military attaché (representative) in London, England.
Once Fuchs began working on the atomic bomb project he
became an active member of the Soviet spy network in America, which was seeking information about atomic research that
could be smuggled into the Soviet Union.

Early in 1944 Anatoli Yakovlev became the head of the
Soviet spy group in the United States while working as a vice-consul (commercial representative) at the Soviet embassy in
New York City. According to a theory that was presented during the Rosenberg trial, Yakovlev's top spies were Harry Gold,
David Greenglass, and Julius and Ethel Rosenberg. Gold was a
Swiss-born Russian immigrant to the United States. In 1935 he
became a Soviet spy, engaging primarily in industrial chemical
theft. Yakovlev appointed Gold to be the go-between with
Fuchs in transmitting information to Kremer in London.
Greenglass, Ethel Rosenberg's brother, had been a member of
the Young Communist League. In spite of his Communist connections, however, he was drafted into the U.S. Army and then
assigned to the Manhattan Project (the team that designed the
atomic bomb) at Oak Ridge, Tennessee, in 1944.

Rosenbergs said to be elite spies

By 1944 Julius Rosenberg had openly been a Communist
for several years. Some historian believe that, using his party
ties, Rosenberg became one of the first espionage agents in the
United States after he obtained important radar secrets before

World War II. After Rosenberg met Ethel Greenglass, he recruited her into the Communist Party and then married her. A bit later, Ethel convinced her brother David to steal classified (top secret) nuclear information when he was transferred to Oak Ridge.

According to certain theorists, after Greenglass took the job at Oak Ridge, the Rosenbergs went underground (concealed their Communist connections). They allegedly worked in conjunction with the three major spy rings operating in the United States at the same time. One was based in New York City. Another was located at the University of California's Radiation Laboratory and linked to the Russian embassy in San Francisco. The third was centered in Chicago, Illinois, where a spy was working as a chemist at the Metallurgical Laboratories, which produced plutonium (a radioactive metallic element) for atomic bombs.

Absolute security

When Yakovlev took over the American spy network, he insisted upon absolute secrecy. This meant the various spy rings had to work independently of one another, thus eliminating the possibility of accidental or deliberate betrayal. Although the Federal Bureau of Investigation (FBI) had learned of individual cases of Soviet espionage in the United States, the U.S. government did not prosecute Soviet spies. And even though the FBI knew about a spy ring in Canada, the agency was totally unaware of the extensive network that had been operating in the United States. Yakovlev's security procedures were successful for three years. During this time Greenglass stole secrets from Oak Ridge and the Rosenbergs allegedly passed along the information to Fuchs. Ironically, the American spy network came undone because of a lapse in security.

Yakovlev's disastrous slip-up

In 1947 the FBI questioned Gold about his spying activities, but he managed to convince the agents that he was not involved in espionage. Then Fuchs was arrested in London. When he confessed and implicated Gold, this connection led back to a slip-up Yakovlev had set in motion in 1945. That year, a few days before the explosion of the first atomic bomb, Greenglass was working at the Los Alamos plant where the bomb was being tested. Greenglass had prepared an extremely important report about the experiments that Yakovlev was anxious to send to Moscow (the Soviet capital). Yakovlev appointed a courier named Ann Sidorovich to pick up Greenglass's report.

For unknown reasons Sidorovich was not able to carry out her assignment. Unwilling to wait until Sidorovich was ready to go to Los Alamos, Yakovlev sent Gold—a courier for Fuchs—in her place. Therefore, when Fuchs was arrested in London he revealed that Gold was his go-between. Gold was then arrested. On the basis of his single trip to Los Alamos, he named Greenglass as a spy within the Manhattan Project. On June 15, 1950, Greenglass confessed to the FBI that he had passed information to Gold. He also claimed he had handed over documents to Ethel and Julius Rosenberg.

Rosenbergs arrested

The next day FBI agents showed up at the Rosenbergs' apartment. Julius told the agents that his brother-in-law was a liar. His refusal to cooperate convinced the FBI that he was hiding something and that they were about to uncover a spy ring of unprecedented importance. Intensifying and broadening its investigation, the bureau found Max Elitcher, a former college classmate of Julius. Elitcher told agents that Rosenberg had approached him various times during the mid-1940s in an attempt to obtain classified information to which Elitcher had access through his work with air force and navy contracts. The FBI concluded it now had its case, and the Rosenbergs were arrested.

Indictment and trial

On August 17, 1950, a federal grand jury indicted (charged with a crime) the Rosenbergs for conspiracy to commit espionage. Lack of direct evidence kept the couple from being charged with treason (betrayal of one's country), a more serious crime. The Rosenbergs' trial began on March 6, 1951. The third defendant was Morton Sobell, whom Elitcher had named as the couple's accomplice (a person who assists in committing a crime). The intense publicity and questionable procedures on the part of prosecutor Irving Saypol prevented the trial from being completely fair. For example, Saypol told the jury that "the evidence of the treasonable acts of these three defendants you will find overwhelming," even though the Rosenbergs and Sobell were not being accused of treason. During the trial Saypol announced in a national news conference that he had secured sworn affidavits (statements) from an old friend of the Rosenbergs named William Perl, statements that conclusively proved the conspiracy. Saypol decided against putting Perl on the witness stand, however, when Perl admitted that he had lied in his affidavits.

Evidence against Rosenbergs

One by one, Greenglass, his wife, Gold, and Elitcher testified that the Rosenbergs were involved in a spy ring. Elitcher admitted, however, that he had never actually passed any documents to Julius. Sobell was never questioned in court, and the Rosenbergs denied any wrongdoing on their part. When Saypol asked them about their past connections with the Communist Party, the couple pleaded the Fifth Amendment and refused to answer. (The Fifth Amendment to the U.S. Constitution guarantees the right of a defendant or a witness in a trial not to testify on the grounds that to do so would be self-incriminating, or suggest guilt.)

A large part of Saypol's case rested on a flight Sobell took to Mexico and Julius Rosenberg's attempt to obtain a passport (a document that permits travel to other countries) after Fuchs

Rosenberg supporters staged picket rallies in Paris, France, and New York City on June 18, 1953.

made his confession. The Rosenbergs' apparent effort to leave the United States confirmed their guilt in the eyes of the jury. After a day of deliberating, the jury found all three defendants guilty of conspiracy.

Sentenced to death

Judge Irving Kaufman had the responsibility of imposing punishment. Although the Rosenbergs and Sobell had not been convicted of treason, Kaufman appeared to pass sentence on unproven acts and a crime for which the defendants had not been charged. Announcing that their crime was "worse than murder," Kaufman declared that "putting into the hands of the Russians the A-bomb has already caused, in my opinion, the communist aggression in Korea [the Korean War, a conflict between communist and non-communist forces from 1950 to 1953], with the resultant casualties exceeding 50,000 and who knows but that millions more innocent people may pay the price of your treason." On April 5, 1951, Kaufman ordered that the Rosenbergs be executed in the electric chair. He sentenced Sobell to thirty years in prison.

Worldwide protests

For two years the Rosenbergs unsuccessfully appealed their convictions, eventually taking their case to the U.S. Supreme Court (the highest court in the United States. The Supreme Court makes the final decision on appealed cases). Meanwhile, public interest in the Rosenbergs' treatment during their trial had reached international proportions. Demonstrators urged the commutation (cancellation) of the couple's death sentences. Some supporters were against the idea of executing a woman, while others protested the hysteria surrounding the trial and the extreme severity of the punishment. Demonstrations in support of the couple were held in Paris, France, and New York City on June 18, 1953. The following evening, shortly before 8:00 P.M., the Rosenbergs were electrocuted in Sing Sing Prison in New York. The couple left behind two young sons, Michael and Robert, who later wrote *We Are Your Sons*, an account of being the children of infamous parents.

Many legal experts continue to claim that the Rosenbergs were victims of a "witch-hunt." The 1950s was an era when public figures such as Senator Joseph McCarthy (see "Society" entry) used scare tactics to fuel the fear of communism. The Rosenbergs therefore became convenient scapegoats in a misguided campaign to purge Communist Party sympathizers from American society.

FOR FURTHER REFERENCE

Books

Meeropol, Robert, and Michael Meeropol. *We Are Your Sons: The Legacy of Ethel and Julius Rosenberg.* Urbana: University of Illinois Press, 1986.

Sharlitt, Joseph F. *Fatal Error: The Miscarriage of Justice That Sealed the Rosenbergs' Fate.* New York City: Scribner's, 1989.

The *Twenty-One* Quiz Show Scandal

1956 TO 1959

The television industry survived the quiz show scandal relatively unscathed.

In 1956 the Soviet Union's launching of *Sputnik,* a small space satellite, raised doubts about the superiority of American public education. In this environment of social uncertainty, Charles Van Doren, a young college instructor and a member of one of America's most prominent intellectual families, became involved in answer-fixing on a quiz show called *Twenty-One.* Van Doren's participation on the show made him one of the first television stars. Each week he demonstrated knowledge about a variety of unrelated topics, leading millions of Americans to watch the show and to root for him to win. When Van Doren finally admitted his complicity in the deception, the effects were devastating for the American public. The willingness of intelligent people to participate in unethical behavior for financial gain and social fame led many observers to ponder the corrupting influence of television. The television industry, however, survived the scandal relatively unscathed.

The $64,000 Question

The first popular television quiz show, *The $64,000 Question,* was created by Lou Cowan, who wanted to prove that the average American could have superior intelligence. The appeal of *The $64,000 Question* was that contestants could use their brains to win large sums of money. As an independent televi-

Jack Barry was the producer of the popular 1950s quiz show *Twenty-One*.

sion producer, Cowan's task was to sell his idea to a sponsor; Cowan and the sponsor would then approach one of the networks. Cowan approached the advertising agency of Revlon, a cosmetics company, which then sold the show to the Columbia Broadcasting System (CBS-TV).

The $64,000 Question debuted in June 1955, and was an immediate hit. The show established its integrity by having the questions delivered to the studio by a bank executive from a locked bank vault. Then an IBM machine selected the questions to be asked in the contestant's specialty area, such as Shakespeare, boxing, or the Bible. The contestant would answer questions of increasing difficulty, with each question worth double the previous total or nothing. At $8,000, the contestant would enter an isolation booth, supposedly in order not to hear audience members yelling out a correct answer. (In fact, the isolation booth's actual purpose was to increase the drama of the show.)

Given the double-or-nothing gamble, one problem the show first faced was that contestants were afraid to compete for $64,000—they often stopped at $32,000. Then, on September 13, 1955, Richard McCutcheon, a marine captain, became the first contestant to win $64,000 when he answered a question in the category of gastronomy (the preparation of food). McCutcheon's question was to name the five dishes and two wines served at a dinner by King George VI of England for President Albert Lebrun in 1939. The big winner was Revlon, however, for the company's sales skyrocketed, jumping fifty-four percent in the show's first six months of sponsorship. By 1958 Revlon was the leader in the cosmetics field.

The Perfect Contestant

The success of *The $64,000 Question* was dependent upon a connection being made between a particular contestant and the television audience. Warm, friendly, attractive contestants were better suited for the requirements of television than those lacking physical and social graces. Through pretesting, a contestant's strengths could be determined (McCutcheon knew French cuisine and not Italian, for example) and played to. Pretested questions could also resemble questions asked on the show. Revlon executives had strong opinions about who made a good contestant and whom they wanted to win. In weekly meetings executives would critique the show, blaming lower ratings on the performances of that week's contestants. For instance, difficult questions were asked of Dr. Joyce Brothers— a psychologist and expert on boxing—because she was disliked by Revlon executives, yet she became the second top winner.

Twenty-One

Other television quiz shows quickly began competing with *The $64,000 Question* for popularity among the American public. Producers Jack Barry and Dan Enright came up with *Twenty-One,* in which two contestants tried to become the first to earn twenty-one points by answering questions of varying difficulty. Placed in isolation booths, the players would not know each other's score, but the television audience would. Barry and Enright were sure they had a winning concept, and they convinced the makers of Geritol, a popular energy supplement, to sponsor *Twenty-One.*

The first *Twenty-One* show, which aired on September 12, 1956, was a flop. Geritol executives became nervous, realizing they could lose money on the show. Martin Rosenhouse, a Geritol representative, told Enright to take whatever steps were necessary to make the show a hit. Enright decided to capitalize on *The $64,000 Question* strategy of promoting good-looking contestants: He would create drama with competition between an attractive hero and an unappealing villain.

The perfect "villain"

Enright found his perfect "villain" in Herbert Stempel, a graduate student at City College of New York. Stempel had written Enright a letter, asking to be a *Twenty-One* contestant. Stempel said he had a photographic memory and therefore had innumerable obscure facts and bits of information at his com-

Academic Charles Van Doren was the perfect *Twenty-One* show contestant: handsome, intelligent, and modest.

mand. On the first test for the show, Stempel answered 251 out of 363 questions correctly, earning the highest score ever. Enright, however, found Stempel not very likable and physically unattractive. Stempel was also socially backward and a poor conversationalist, so he clearly would not project a positive image on television. Enright decided to exploit this fact by having Stempel wear old, ill-fitting clothes and a short, military-style haircut. Enright then took the next step: He gave Stempel the answers he did not know, thus setting him up to win several times before being defeated by a more appealing contestant. Enticing Stempel with the guarantee of winning $25,000, Enright made him an unwitting coconspirator in one of the biggest scams in entertainment history.

The perfect "hero"

In spite of his lack of social skills and unkempt appearance, Stempel became a television celebrity. Enright and his deputy, Al Freedman, then set out to find a "hero" who would defeat Stempel in a dramatic confrontation on the show. Freedman thought he had found the perfect candidate: Charles Van Doren, a literature instructor at Columbia University. Van Doren, however, was not initially agreeable to Freedman's offer, saying he enjoyed teaching and had no interest in television. During a number of luncheon meetings, Freedman persisted in trying to change Van Doren's mind.

Enright and Freeman knew that everyone was vain in some way; for Van Doren it turned out to be his love of teaching. Freedman wore Van Doren down by telling him that he could improve the status of teachers by winning on the show. But Van Doren wondered how Freedman knew that he would win. Freedman responded by saying that in show business, truth takes on a different meaning. He gave the example of President Dwight D. Eisenhower's having recently published a book under his own name when in fact it had been ghostwritten. Still, Van Doren was not convinced, and he asked Freedman how much money he could win. Up to $100,000, Freedman answered. Before Van Doren committed himself, he asked Freedman if anyone else would know about the deception, and Freedman vowed absolute secrecy. Finally, Van Doren agreed to appear on *Twenty-One*.

Stempel agrees to lose

Enright told Stempel he was going to lose to Van Doren on December 5, 1956. Unhappy with this prospect, Stempel asked if he could play against Van Doren fairly, but Enright said no. Stempel agreed to the fix, but he became troubled when Enright told him that he had to miss a question about the title of the movie that won the Academy Award for Best Picture in 1955. The answer was *Marty,* a film Stempel had seen a number of times. This turn of events proved to be humiliating for Stempel, who knew he had made a fool of himself by "forgetting" the title of one of his favorite movies. Although he had agreed to go along with the arrangement, he became fixated on the experience. Years later, Stempel wondered how different history would have been if he had given the right answer.

Van Doren is ideal contestant

Van Doren was successful beyond anyone's imaginings. Sincere, attractive, and modest, he projected a perfect television image and he responded well to Freedman's coaching on mannerisms to use when giving answers. Each week an adoring public sent Van Doren thousands of letters praising his brilliant performance against contestants who were never quite able to beat him. But Stempel hated him, knowing his fame was based on a lie—just as Stempel's own fame had been a fraud—and this hatred never abated. The adulation continued for Van Doren as he won in a record fifteen appearances. Although he was offered jobs at other universities and even in the movies, he signed a contract with the National Broadcasting System (NBC) to make regular appearances on the *Today* television show for $50,000 a year. Finally it was time for Van Doren to be defeated. Before losing to a contestant named Vivienne Nearing, he had won $129,000 (although he paid $101,000 in taxes).

Master of ceremonies Jack Barry (behind podium) smiles at contestant Elizabeth Anderson during the final broadcast of *Twenty-One* on October 16, 1958.

Stempel seeks revenge

Deeply angered by Van Doren's popularity, Stempel wanted to hurt his successful opponent, even if it meant destroying his own reputation. Enright had counted on everyone agreeing to a conspiracy of silence, but Stempel no longer cared about protecting himself. He confronted Enright, who trapped him by tape-recording a conversation in which Stempel tried to

| Great Misadventures

blackmail him. As Stempel spun out of control, he went to the press and then to the district attorney, telling everyone how Enright and Freedman had cleverly fixed *Twenty-One*.

Stempel's claims, however, could not be proved. Enright and Freedman had carefully planned the scam so there were no witnesses besides the contestants, who were themselves co-conspirators. Daily newspapers, resentful of television competition, nevertheless made Stempel's charges a major, continuing story. Barry and Enright sold the show to NBC for $2 million in 1957, but nothing deterred Stempel. He continued to make his apparently dangerous claims without corroboration until a former *Twenty-One* contestant found a notebook of another contestant that contained correct answers. Then another disgruntled contestant came forward, revealing that he, too, had been coached by Enright and Freedman—but he had also taken the unusual precaution of sending the answers to himself through registered mail. The district attorney's office now had concrete proof of rigging, yet the judge in the case impounded (seized) the evidence.

Congress enters investigation

At that time a congressional committee was in the process of investigating television quiz show fixing. But they were not easily convinced by evidence from former *Twenty-One* contestants. Heading the staff investigation was Richard N. Goodwin, a young lawyer who had graduated first in his class at Harvard Law School and had clerked with Supreme Court Justice Felix Frankfurter. When Goodwin first met Stempel, he could relate to Stempel's background and desire to get ahead; Goodwin did not, however, understand Stempel's overwhelming animosity toward Van Doren.

While Goodwin was gathering information about television quiz shows for the committee, he became acquainted with Van Doren and grew to admire him as an exceptional person. The two men developed a friendship through their shared interests in literature and culture. Van Doren protested his innocence to Goodwin, and Goodwin, knowing the evidence showed otherwise, wanted to believe in Van Doren. Yet he finally had to acknowledge that Van Doren had indeed been implicated in the *Twenty-One* scam. Goodwin planned to avoid making Van Doren appear before the committee because it would seem too much like a McCarthy-era hearing. Van Doren, however, did a stupid thing: In order to keep his job on the *Today* show, he sent a telegram to the committee stating his innocence. His fate was now sealed—he had to testify.

Van Doren's statement

Van Doren appeared before the congressional committee on November 2, 1959. Reading from a prepared statement, he admitted that he had been involved in the *Twenty-One* deception. In fact, he confessed to taking the side of evil in a battle with good, and he apologized for disappointing millions of people. Van Doren's dramatic speech made a profound impression on the committee, and individual members praised him for his courage. Then Congressman Steve Derounian announced that he was not going to congratulate Van Doren for admitting an obvious truth, and the audience broke into applause. The adoration of Van Doren was over. After he lost his job at Columbia, Van Doren moved with his wife, Geraldine Bernstein Van Doren, to Chicago, Illinois, where they later raised two children. Withdrawing from public life, he began working for Encyclopedia Britannica. Van Doren never spoke publicly about his involvement in the quiz show scandal and repeatedly refused to answer reporters' questions.

The *Twenty-One* scandal was the basis of the critically-acclaimed 1994 film *Quiz Show*, directed by Robert Redford. Starring Ralph Fiennes as Charles Van Doren and John Turturro as Herbert Stempel, the film won recognition for its accurate depiction on corporate greed, class rivalry, and the power of television. The screenplay was adapted from *Remembering America: A Voice from the Sixties* by Goodwin.

FOR FURTHER REFERENCE

Books

Halberstam, David. *The Fifties*. New York City: Villard Books, 1993, pp. 643–66.

The Watergate Cover-Up

1972 TO 1974

Revelations about the

Watergate break-in led

to the first resignation

of a president in

American history.

At 2:00 A.M. on Saturday, June 17, 1972, five men were arrested while burglarizing the offices of the Democratic National Committee (DNC) located in the Watergate apartment complex in Washington, D.C. One of the men, James McCord, was a member of the Committee to Reelect the President (CREEP). The presence of McCord immediately raised suspicions of political intrigue. The following Monday, Ron Ziegler, the spokesman for President Richard M. Nixon (1913–1996), dismissed the break-in as nothing more than a "third-rate burglary." As events continued to unfold over the next few months, this "ordinary" burglary exploded into a full-fledged scandal.

Later referred to as "Watergate," the burglary eventually led to the first resignation of a president in American history. Subsequent congressional hearings also exposed a dark underside of politics and resulted in the appointment of a permanent special prosecutor charged with investigating wrongdoing in the executive branch of the U.S. government. Public cynicism about politics has had a profound impact on each American president who has been in office since Nixon resigned in disgrace in 1974.

Reasons for Watergate unclear

Until scholars gain full access to President Richard M. Nixon's personal papers and tapes, the full story of the Watergate break-in—especially who ordered it and why—will remain unclear. Nevertheless, public documents provide some clues. Prior to the burglary of the DNC offices, the Nixon administration had already engaged in illegal harassment and surveillance of its political opponents. In addition, Nixon associates often preferred operating secretly rather than conducting policy publicly.

The most crucial clue, however, is that in early 1972 (when the Watergate affair was set in motion), Nixon was unsure of his prospects for reelection. The general theory is that members of the Committee to Reelect the President hatched plots to wiretap offices of both the Democratic presidential nominee George McGovern (1922–) and the Democratic National Committee chairman Lawrence O'Brien. Both attempts failed. The Watergate burglary actually involved the second CREEP break-in at O'Brien's office (the burglars were trying to replace a defective listening device). It is also known that, six days following the arrests, Nixon directed his staff to hinder a Federal Bureau of Investigation (FBI) inquiry into the case. He also ordered a cover-up of the connections between the burglars and CREEP. This was the first of many attempts by the most powerful law enforcement official in the United States to obstruct justice.

As a result of the Watergate affair, Richard M. Nixon became the first American president to resign from office.

Reporters and judge bring pressure

President Nixon had ordered a cover-up because he feared that an investigation into the break-in would expose various illegal activities committed by his administration. During the 1972 election, Democrats who charged that Watergate represented wider political crimes were dismissed as being partisan (prejudiced by party loyalty). The break-in had no effect on Nixon's campaign, and he was reelected for a second term in an historic landslide victory. The story would have died were it not for the criminal trial of the Watergate burglars and for two intrepid reporters from *The Washington Post,* Bob Woodward

Federal judge John J. Sirica presided over the criminal trial of the Watergate burglars.

and Carl Bernstein. Woodward and Bernstein continued to dig into the case. Together with John J. Sirica, the federal judge overseeing the criminal trial, the reporters kept pressure on the White House, demanding an explanation of the break-in and the connection between CREEP and James McCord.

The White House desperately sought to isolate McCord and suggest to the public that he or his superiors in CREEP ordered the break-in without the president's knowledge. CREEP immediately distanced itself from McCord, even as it secretly paid his legal fees. Files were destroyed, and hush money was offered to people involved in the case. Unmistakable evidence nonetheless pointed to the fact that someone high up in the administration had authorized Watergate. Gradually, connections between the burglars and their superiors in CREEP were disclosed. Eventually these links were traced from members of CREEP to the White House staff.

White House staff implicated

As the investigation moved closer to the White House, members of Nixon's staff tried to protect themselves from criminal prosecution. Resignations became commonplace. CREEP chairman John Mitchell and CREEP treasurer Hugh Sloan left in the fall of 1972. White House chief of staff H.R. Haldeman, domestic policy assistant John Ehrlichman, presidential counsel John Dean, and Attorney General Richard Kleindienst all resigned on April 30, 1973. McCord informed Sirica that members of the Nixon administration had perjured themselves (lied under oath) during his criminal trial.

No one in the conspiracy was willing to take the blame for the crime. The question reporters Woodward and Bernstein sought to answer was: How much did the president know, and when did he know it? The Democrats and the Congress also wanted to know the answer to that question. On February 7,

1973, the U.S. Senate voted seventy to zero to establish a seven-member committee, headed by Senator Samuel J. Ervin (1896–1985), to probe the Watergate case. Immediately following his triumphant second inauguration, Nixon was fighting for his political life.

Public transfixed by Watergate

Throughout 1973 Americans were transfixed by the Watergate affair. The criminal trial of the Watergate burglars was taking place, and the Ervin committee was conducting its investigations. Woodward and Bernstein were publishing sensational reports in the *Washington Post* based on information from a secret source inside the Nixon administration whom they called "Deep Throat." A special prosecutor (an attorney with the power to take legal action), Archibald Cox, had also been authorized by the Justice Department to study Watergate without interference from the White House.

John Mitchell, a former attorney general and the chairman of the Committee to Reelect the President (CREEP), was placed on trial for campaign financing violations.

A media frenzy ensued as these simultaneous investigations produced startling revelations on an almost daily basis. The Ervin committee's televised hearings climaxed in the stunning testimony of White House counsel Dean, who made statements that implicated the president in the Watergate cover-up. Even more damaging was the public testimony of White House aide Alexander Butterfield. Butterfield revealed the existence of a secret recording system installed in the White House. Unbelievably, presidential decisions regarding Watergate had been recorded on tape.

Showdown over tapes

Ervin, Cox, and Sirica immediately pressed the White House to turn over the Watergate tapes. Nixon rejected these requests. Claiming the tapes were private property, he asserted that they contained material that might compromise national security. Nixon further argued that he had a right to

White House presidential counsel John Dean (behind desk with hand raised) is sworn in before giving testimony at the Senate Watergate Committee hearings.

withhold the tapes under the constitutional claim of "executive privilege"—an idea that the president could decide for himself how much he might cooperate with other branches of the government.

Nixon's rationalizations were a public relations disaster. The press charged the president with "stonewalling," or preventing access to the truth of the Watergate affair. The president's popularity plummeted twenty-eight points in the polls, to below forty percent. When the Ervin committee offered to review the tapes privately, Nixon still refused. When prosecutor Cox and judge Sirica subpoenaed seven of the tapes, the president challenged their authority to investigate the White House.

The "Saturday Night Massacre"

On October 12, the U.S. District Circuit Court of Appeals ordered Nixon to turn over the subpoenaed Watergate tapes to Cox and Sirica. The president responded by offering to release prepared transcripts of the tapes. His decision infuriated Cox, who attacked the administration for noncompliance. Nixon then ordered Attorney General Elliot Richardson to fire Cox. Richardson refused, saying he had promised the Senate in his confirmation hearing that he would not interfere with the special prosecutor. Nixon then fired Richardson, and ordered Deputy Attorney General William Ruckelhaus to fire Cox. Ruckelhaus also refused, and Nixon fired Ruckelhaus. Nixon finally persuaded Solicitor General Robert Bork to dismiss Cox. The FBI then moved in and sealed off the offices of Cox, Richardson, and Ruckelhaus.

The public was outraged by these actions. The press termed the firings the "Saturday Night Massacre." Calls for Nixon's impeachment rang through Congress. Nixon's popularity rating dropped to an unprecedented low of twenty-two percent. Even worse for Nixon, the negative public response insured that the new attorney general, William Saxbe (former senator from Ohio), and new special prosecutor, Leon Jaworski (a lawyer from Texas), could not appear to be even slightly favorable to the administration. Saxbe and Jaworski continued the vigorous investigative methods of Richardson and Cox.

The White House transcripts

By the end of October, Nixon still had not complied with court orders for the tapes. In fact, he announced that two of the tapes did not even exist. Critics then charged Nixon with destroying evidence. The charges became more plausible after Nixon revealed a mysterious gap in another of the subpoenaed tapes. Nixon's secretary, Rose Mary Woods, claimed that she had accidentally erased more than eighteen minutes of the tape in question. Her explanation only confirmed the suspicions of those who were afraid Nixon would tamper with the tapes in his possession.

In an effort to turn the tide of public opinion, on April 29, 1974, Nixon released a 1,308-page edited transcript of the Watergate tapes. He maintained that the transcripts proved he knew nothing about the Watergate cover-up until March 21, 1973. Nixon hoped he had restored public confidence in his truthfulness. Instead, the transcripts, with "expletive deleted" peppered across the pages, embarrassed the president and made him the object of ridicule.

Prosecutions and convictions of high officials

Indictments and convictions for criminal wrongdoing further eroded the president's public support. McCord and G. Gordon Liddy, his superior at CREEP, were convicted in January 1974. The other four men who had burglarized the DNC offices were also convicted. The following spring White House aides Charles Colson and Ehrlichman were found guilty of conspiracy and burglary for breaking into the office of Daniel Ellsberg's psychiatrist. CREEP official Dwight Chapin was sent to prison for his role in covering up the "dirty tricks" campaign. White House counsel Dean was found guilty of conspiracy and began to cooperate with prosecutors. Former attorney general Mitchell and CREEP official Maurice Stans were placed on trial for campaign financing violations, while former Texas governor John Connally was investigated for similar activities.

Vice President Spiro T. Agnew, who so often made law and order the theme of his speeches, was investigated by the Justice Department for criminal charges unrelated to Watergate. On October 10, 1973, Agnew resigned the vice presidency and pleaded no contest to one count of income tax evasion. In return for the plea, the Justice Department dropped other counts of bribery and extortion associated with Agnew's tenure as governor of Maryland. Finally, on March 1, 1974, special prosecutor Jaworski secured from a federal grand jury indictments for obstruction of justice against seven Nixon aides—including Mitchell, Haldeman, and Ehrlichman.

Impeachment proceedings begin

The grand jury found Nixon to be an "unindicted coconspirator" because Jaworski doubted that a sitting president was subject to criminal indictment by a grand jury. According to the United States Constitution, only Congress can indict a president for criminal wrongdoing, a process known as impeachment. During impeachment proceedings, the House of Representatives determines whether a indictment is justified, then the chief justice of the Supreme Court presides over a trial, with the Senate acting as a jury. If the president is found guilty of high crimes or misdemeanors, he can be removed from office.

By now, impeachment of the president was a real possibility. Judge Sirica turned over Watergate evidence to the House Judiciary Committee, which had been impaneled to draw up articles of impeachment to be voted upon by the full House of Representatives. Committee chairman Peter Rodino, a Democrat from New Jersey, sifted through the evidence with meticulous care and the assistance of politically independent attorney John Doar. Rodino and Doar concluded that a conversation Nixon had with Haldeman on June 23, 1972, would reveal whether or not the president had obstructed justice.

The two men then subpoenaed Nixon for the tape of that conversation (among others). The president refused to cooperate, however, again citing "executive privilege" and the already-published White House transcripts. It was left to the Supreme Court to decide the merit of Nixon's claim. On July 24, 1974, in *The United States vs. Richard Nixon,* the court unanimously upheld the constitutionality of executive privilege. Deciding that the principle did not apply to the Watergate tapes, however, the justices ordered Nixon to turn over all subpoenaed tapes to Jaworski. On July 30, the House Judiciary Committee recommended to the full House that it vote to impeach the president for three offenses: obstruction of justice, abuse of power, and contempt of Congress.

First U.S. president to resign

With the Supreme Court ruling against him and the House about to vote on his impeachment, Nixon was trapped. On August 5, transcripts of the June 23 conversation became available to the public. The "smoking gun" Nixon's supporters feared, the conversation proved the president had ordered a cover-up. Nixon's defenders were stunned, and leading Republicans went to the White House to report that the president had lost all congressional support. On August 8, 1974, in a televised address, Nixon announced that he was resigning from office, effective at noon the following day. Vice President Gerald R. Ford (1913–), who had assumed his office after Agnew resigned, became the thirty-eighth president of the United States.

On September 8, 1974, Ford granted Nixon a "full, free and absolute pardon" to spare the former president the indignity of undergoing a criminal prosecution for obstruction of justice. Within a week Ford's popularity fell from seventy-one percent to forty-nine percent—the largest single drop in polling history. Ford's political career never recovered.

Aftermath of Watergate

At his inaugural, President Ford announced an end to "our long national nightmare." But Watergate and its effect on American political life did not easily disappear. Nixon had repeatedly charged that the crimes of his administration were no different from the activities of previous (Democratic) presidencies. Investigators and historians later substantiated these charges: Presidents John F. Kennedy (1917–1963) and Lyndon B. Johnson (1908–1973) had also made secret tapes, profited from their offices, and engaged in dirty political tricks. Along with Watergate, these revelations caused a new public cynicism toward politics, which was reflected in increasing voter apathy. By the 1990s character had become the foremost issue in presidential politics.

FOR FURTHER REFERENCE

Books

Bernstein, Carl, and Bob Woodward. *All the President's Men.* New York City: Simon & Schuster, 1974; reprinted 1994.

Herda, D. J. *United States vs. Nixon: Watergate and the President.* New York City: Enslow Publishers, 1996.

Big-Budget Movie Mania

1977 TO PRESENT

By establishing big budgets as the norm, film studios set financial goals that became harder and harder to reach.

During the late 1970s a Hollywood trend was started with the phenomenal success of the movie *Star Wars* (1977), the most profitable film in history up to that time. (George Lucas (1944–), the film's director, reportedly made a personal profit of $50 million.) *Star Wars* was followed by *The Empire Strikes Back* (1980) and *Return of the Jedi* (1983), two sequel films that were also huge money makers. Based on the monetary success of the "Star Wars" trilogy, studios and producers realized that high-risk commercial motion pictures—if developed and packaged carefully—had the potential to return previously unheard-of profits.

By the early 1980s major Hollywood studios were investing millions of dollars in big-budget moviemaking. In order to guarantee a "built-in" audience, films were often based on well-known subjects, like best-selling books and popular television shows. In other instances, however, studios backed directors' "pet projects," films with sometimes questionable financial potential. Whether based on an existing subject or a director's original concept, however, these big-budget projects often backfired, leading to financial and artistic disaster. Three films are especially representative of this trend: *Heaven's Gate* (1981), *The Bonfire of the Vanities* (1990), and *Waterworld* (1995). Cost overruns, schedule delays, and negative press reports plagued these movies. As a result, the studios lost more money than they could ever hope to make on the projects. Ironically, by establishing big budgets as the norm, the studios had set financial goals that became harder and harder to reach.

High hopes for *Heaven's Gate*

Heaven's Gate is an example of how one bad film can ruin a director's career and hurt a studio's bottom line. In 1978 Michael Cimino (1943–) won an Academy Award as best director for *The Deer Hunter*, a film that portrays the experiences of working-class men fighting in the Vietnam War (see "Military" entry). Hollywood producers (business people who provide money for making movies) were banking on Cimino's previous success when they chose him to direct *Heaven's Gate* for the United Artists studio the following year.

The plot of this epic Western was expected to have huge popular appeal. *Heaven's Gate* was based on the true story of bloody wars between cattlemen and immigrant settlers in Johnson County, Wyoming, in 1892. To help re-create the story, Cimino assembled a huge cast with well-known stars in the lead roles. Among these stars was Christopher Walken, who had earned an Academy Award for his performance in *The Deer Hunter*. Walken played Nathan D. Champion, a gunfighter hired by the ranchers. Cimino picked country singer-songwriter Kris Kristofferson to appear as James Averill, the marshal who must intervene between the two hostile groups. In spite of the potentially winning combination of a great director and prominent actors, however, *Heaven's Gate* became a monumental failure.

Cimino a perfectionist

From the start the film was plagued by delays and cost overruns. The entire project was budgeted at $11.5 million, but Cimino spent an average of $200,000 a day, to bring the final total to $44 million. (In late 1990s dollars this figure would be close to $100 million.) The director was a perfectionist who thought nothing of spending whatever was required to get the effect he wanted. For instance, Cimino rebuilt trains to achieve authentic nineteenth-century detail, and he ordered that extras (people who appear in crowd scenes

A scene from the 1981 film *Heaven's Gate*. Obsessed with re-creating a Wyoming town circa 1892, director Michael Cimino rebuilt trains, planted new grass, and made sure that even the extras' clothing was in perfect period detail.

or in background roles) should be costumed as if they were lead characters. In one case, Cimino even planted miles of sod (carpet-like strips of grass with soil attached, used for making lawns) only to blow up the expensive investment in a battlefield scene. Cimino also filmed scenes over and over until they met his satisfaction. Because of the director's recent Academy Award, studio executives were at first afraid to interfere. Alarmed by ballooning expenses and increasing delays, they finally intervened. It was too late, however, to salvage the costly project.

Film sets dubious record

In spite of unfavorable publicity about the film that had been circulating for months, United Artists decided to release *Heaven's Gate* anyway. Running three hours and thirty-nine minutes, the movie opened at a gala premier in New York City on November 18, 1980. The response was overwhelmingly negative: Critics loudly and unanimously pronounced the film a flop. The next day Cimino and United Artists pulled the movie out of circulation.

As a result, *Heaven's Gate* now holds the distinction of being the only movie to be withdrawn from theaters immediately after being released. In an attempt to salvage at least some of their investment, Cimino and the producers decided to shorten the running time of the film to two hours and thirty minutes. They then set a second release date for five months later. These efforts, however, were futile—the film was still a failure at the box office. Ironically, the original version of *Heaven's Gate* (called the "director's cut") was released in England in 1983 to critical acclaim. The director's cut met even greater praise six years later in Paris, France, where it was regarded as a masterpiece.

In the United States, however, Cimino's career was tarnished almost beyond repair. He was given fewer and fewer chances to direct major motion pictures. In 1997, for example, Cimino made *Sunchaser,* the story of two men who roam the American West in search of the meaning of life. The film had only a limited run in theaters before being shown on cable television.

The Bonfire of the Vanities causes controversy

The Bonfire of the Vanities is another famous misadventure in moviemaking. The film was based on a 1987 bestselling novel by journalist Tom Wolfe. *The Bonfire of the Vanities* tells the story of Sherman McCoy, a Wall Street bond (certificate of investment) salesman, whose life is dramatically changed by a wrong turn on a dark street. One night McCoy picks up his mistress, Maria, at the airport. On the way back to Manhattan, the couple gets lost in Harlem. Maria then accidentally backs the car over a young man and seriously injures him. Sherman and Maria flee the scene of the accident. Within a few days the car is traced to McCoy and he is arrested. The trial is McCoy's undoing, as he loses his job, money, and wife. Brian De Palma (1940–), a top Hollywood director, was chosen to make the film version of *The Bonfire of the Vanities* for the Warner Brothers studio. An all-star cast, headed by Tom Hanks as Sherman and Melanie Griffith as Maria, was selected for major and minor roles. Everyone involved in the project predicted that the movie would be a big success.

Soon after filming began in New York City, however, the production ran into problems. The trouble started in a mostly black and Hispanic area of the Bronx (a part of New York City), where Sherman and Maria's hit-and-run scene was scheduled to be filmed. Initially, Bronx residents welcomed the actors and crew, but then they became concerned about the negative portrayal of their neighborhood. Fernando Ferrer, president of the Bronx borough, threatened to lead a boycott of Warner Brothers if the studio did not create a more positive image for the area. Finally New York mayor David Dinkins entered the debate and supported the right of the film makers to depict the Bronx in any way they wished. After that controversy had died down, New Jersey chief justice Robert Wilentz refused to allow a production crew to film a scene at his Essex County courthouse in Newark, New Jersey. Objecting to a segment of the scene in which black citizens riot outside the courthouse, the justice demanded changes in the script. A state court judge ultimately overruled Wilentz's order and permitted filming to proceed.

Bonfire flawed by changes

The Bonfire of the Vanities was finally released in December 1990. The movie's budget was huge—around $50 million—but Warner Brothers still expected to make $100 million or more on the finished product. After all, the film had a recognizable story, an acclaimed director, and some of the most famous stars in show business. Bonfire, however, earned a mere $15.6 million at the box office. It failed primarily because critics and moviegoers did not like the changes that director De Palma made to the plot and characters. In one of many errors in casting, the character of Peter Fallow, a journalist for a British tabloid (a sensationalist newspaper), became an American who was played by actor Bruce Willis. De Palma turned Fallow into the movie's hero by having him write a bestselling book about McCoy's trial. This was a major departure from the novel, in which Fallow was just one of many self-interested characters who could not be trusted.

De Palma also faced charges of prejudice when he removed actor Alan Arkin from the role of a Jewish trial judge and replaced him with African American actor Morgan Freeman. This change canceled out one of the main points Wolfe made in his book—that the legal system is run by whites who decide the fates of blacks. Summing up the sentiments of most people who saw *The Bonfire of the Vanities*, critic David Denby remarked in *New York* magazine that the film had "already become a famous disaster."

Waterworld depicts frightening future

Waterworld was perhaps the most ambitious film misadventure of all time. As the star of the film, actor Kevin Costner (1955–) was attempting to duplicate the success he had achieved in 1990 with *Dances with Wolves*, in which he was both the lead actor and director. For *Waterworld* Costner teamed with his director friend Kevin Reynolds, who had also directed *Robin Hood, Prince of Thieves* in 1991. *Waterworld* is set in the future after a natural disaster. Polar icecaps have melted, possibly because of the greenhouse effect (a warming of the Earth's surface and atmosphere), and water has flooded the entire world. The survivors live on floating atolls (coral islands) searching for fresh water and edible food. The Atollers are terrorized by the cigarette-

Actor and director Kevin Costner starred in *Waterworld*, an expensive epic about a futuristic world totally covered with water.

addicted Smokers. This band of outlaws is led by Dennis Hopper as the Deacon.

Arriving in this landless world is Costner as the Mariner, a sailor who expertly navigates a trimaran (a fast sailboat with three hulls side by side). The Mariner is an outsider who shuns human contact because he is a "muto," a human with tiny gills behind his ears and webbed feet that he usually keeps hidden. The Mariner becomes involved in a series of adventures that pit him against the Smokers and the Deacon. The film culminates in the Mariner's rescue of a girl named Enola and her mother and their arrival on dry land.

Waterworld sets cost record

Financed by Universal Pictures studios, *Waterworld* was the most expensive film ever made. According to most accounts, it ended up costing over $240 million—nearly five

DANCES WITH WOLVES STARTS TREND

In a five-year period, from 1987 to 1992, Kevin Costner starred in a series of box office hits: *The Untouchables* (1987), *Bull Durham* (1988), *Field of Dreams* (1989), *Dances with Wolves* (1990), *Robin Hood, Prince of Thieves* (1991), and *The Bodyguard* (1992). Even more remarkably, Costner was both star and director of *Dances With Wolves*, which won seven Academy Awards, including the award for best director. *Dances with Wolves* changed Hollywood's perception of the relationship between box office potential and movie length. Earning $364 million worldwide, the film showed that movies running three hours or longer could still be highly profitable. Earlier films had exceeded three hours and also enjoyed great success. Among these movies were *Gone with the Wind* (1939), *Dr. Zhivago* (1965), and the three "Godfather" movies. In the 1990s three other long films won Academy Awards: *Schindler's List* (1993), *Braveheart* (1995), and *Titanic* (1997). Nevertheless, giving directors the freedom to make very long films always had the potential to backfire in many ways, as demonstrated by *Waterworld*.

times the budget for *Heaven's Gate*. Cost overruns caused negative publicity, which ruined any chance of the film's succeeding in the United States. Perhaps the biggest expenditure resulted from the difficulty of shooting a movie almost entirely on water. (*Waterworld* was filmed in the Pacific Ocean, off the coast of Hawaii.)

No one had anticipated this problem in the planning stages. For instance, three hundred workers took three months to build the main set, a one thousand-ton structure that later sank to the bottom of the ocean. For six weeks of the eight-month filming schedule, 425 extras and crew members had to be ferried to a floating atoll one thousand yards from land. Strong winds, clouds, and humpback whales constantly interrupted the project. A ten-minute action scene took a month to shoot. Even on calm days, scenes had to be re-shot repeatedly so that camera angles could be matched in the editing process. (After film is shot it is taken to an editing room where it is cut and reassembled for the desired effect. Angles from which cameras take pictures must therefore be exact so the final image will fit together.) If things were not bad enough, Reynolds quit when he discovered that Costner was editing the film behind his back. Costner was therefore left to finish the job himself, just three months before *Waterworld* was set for release.

International box office success

Despite these problems *Waterworld* opened in American theaters on July 28, 1995. The film ultimately earned only $88 million. Most of this money came from other countries, where audiences greeted the futuristic tale more enthusiastically. Observers unanimously agreed, however, that enough tickets could never be sold to recover the huge losses resulting from the project. Costner continued to make films. In 1997 he directed and starred in *The Postman,* a movie that is strikingly similar to *Waterworld.* Set in the year 2013 and filmed in Oregon, the movie takes place in the United States after a devastating war. A heroic former postal worker (Costner) defends bewildered survivors against the forces of destruction. Like *Waterworld, The Postman* was considered a failure in the United States, although it was fairly well received overseas.

Titanic—an unexpected success

The 1997 movie *Titanic* was beset by problems similar to those that doomed *Heaven's Gate, The Bonfire of the Vanities,* and *Waterworld.* The story of the tragic sinking of the world's largest passenger ship in 1912 (see "Science and Technology" entry), *Titanic* threatened to become a disaster. The film's director, James Cameron (1954–), built a replica of the luxury ocean liner for the movie set. He also insisted on faithful reproduction of even the most minute period details in costumes, interior furnishings, and other aspects of the production.

The press constantly criticized Cameron's cost overruns, and Hollywood observers often depicted the director as a self-indulgent tyrant. Eventually the film's budget topped $200 million, threatening to rival *Waterworld* as the most expensive movie on record. Unlike its predecessors, however, *Titanic* turned out to be the most successful film in history, bringing in over one billion dollars worldwide in only three months. It also went on to win eleven Academy Awards, including best picture and best director of 1997.

Money becomes the issue

Titanic's overwhelming success came as a surprise to just about everyone involved. The film's production costs were so great that two studios had to underwrite the project. Director Cameron waived both his director and production fees to help keep expenses in line. *Titanic's* length—over three hours—made the film's distributors very nervous, largely because this limited the number of times the movie could be shown in theaters every day. Even after *Titanic* won its many awards, critics still were questioning the wisdom of spending so much money on such a big gamble.

In recent years, studios have found themselves financing more and more "event" movies. As film budgets have grown, however, profit margins have become smaller. Unlike the *Star Wars* era, consumers now have more entertainment options than ever available to them. As a result, film studios are finding it harder and harder to entice moviegoers into theaters. Many recent "event" movies have failed to find either an audience or a warm critical reception. In a rather ironic twist, in recent years both the low-budget independent and the "art house" film markets have seen their popularity—and profits—grow.

FOR FURTHER REFERENCE

Periodicals

Denby, David. "Movies." *New York.* January 7, 1991, pp. 64–65.

Denver International Airport Construction

1984 TO 1995

A t the time it began full operation in 1995, the Denver International Airport (DIA) in Colorado became the first new major airport to open in the United States in over twenty years. Featuring mechanical innovations in an environmentally conscious design, the DIA was a stunning architectural masterpiece. For several years, however, the airport seemed destined to become a huge failure. When the airport was first proposed, controversy arose over its location—a forty-minute drive from downtown Denver and miles away from hotels. After the site was approved, other serious concerns were raised. Engineers claimed the soil was too unstable to support runways, while Native Americans protested that the land was sacred ground. Once the DIA was under construction, the project ran nearly $4 billion over budget and completion was delayed four times. The major problem was a $232 million baggage system that never worked. In spite of this troubled history, the completed DIA has impressed many former critics with its smooth operation and future growth potential.

In spite of a troubled financial and mechanical history, the completed Denver International Airport has impressed many former critics with its smooth operation and future growth potential.

A costly venture

The DIA project was initiated in 1984, while Federico Peña was the mayor of Denver. When Peña took office in 1983, he opposed building a new airport. He favored expanding the existing airport, Stapleton International, which was only a twenty-minute drive from the city and more conveniently situated near hotels. The new airport, on the other hand, would involve twice the driving time—forty minutes—and would be located miles away from lodging accommodations. Other powerful officials, however, wanted a new facility because they believed it would make money. Finally, Pena decided to approve the venture.

According to early plans, Denver International would feature the latest in aviation facility technology. It would also be very expensive, so Pena had to work hard to convince Denver citizens that the DIA needed to be built. He and his administration also had to win grants (sums of money given to support a particular project) from the state and federal governments. Officials at both levels of government generally supported the DIA venture, telling citizens that the airport would stimulate the economy. Voters eventually agreed to the project in 1989, and many Denver businesses offered financing. The DIA was going to be so costly, however, that Pena had to go to even greater lengths and raise funds among the city's wealthiest citizens.

Opening delayed and delayed

Pena left office in 1991 and formed his own business, Pena Investment Advisors. (He was appointed U.S. Secretary of Transportation by President Bill Clinton in 1992.) Wellington Webb was elected the new mayor of Denver. By now the necessary funds had been raised and construction was under way on the DIA, which was scheduled to open on October 31, 1993. Almost as soon as the project began, however, it was plagued by numerous problems such as poor construction, the deaths of two workers, mismanagement, cost overruns, and charges of fraud. Nevertheless, a gala celebration, with 1,300 dignitaries and guests in attendance, was held to inaugurate the new facility on Halloween Day, 1993.

The DIA did not open in 1993, nor was it doing business a year later. The innovative automatic baggage-handling system repeatedly failed to work, and the only alternative was to keep the airport closed until the system was fixed. The opening was postponed three more times, to the great embarrassment of the city of Denver. By then the DIA had become the object of jokes throughout the country. Finally, the airport opened its doors on

February 28, 1995, over sixteen months after the originally scheduled date. Once the airport was in operation, however, the baggage system still would not function properly. After more than $1 million in repairs, the most advanced baggage-handling apparatus in the world had to be replaced by an old-fashioned model.

DIA under investigation

By that time the DIA project had come under the intense scrutiny of six separate agencies: the Federal Bureau of Investigation (FBI), the Securities and Exchange Commission (SEC), the Justice Department, the General Accounting Office (GAO), the Senate Banking Committee, and the Denver district attorney's office. The largest investigation was started by the SEC immediately after the DIA opened. The SEC had received complaints about fraudulent (dishonest) practices by Denver officials, including Pena and Webb.

The most controversial issue was whether or not Pena and Webb failed to disclose important information about the project to bondholders. (Bondholders are investors who purchase certificates, or bonds, that pay interest. Interest is an additional amount of money based on a percentage of the purchase price. Bonds are commonly sold to fund public projects.) For instance, officials knew the baggage-handling system did not work, but they did not tell the bondholders about this and other setbacks. On February 28, the day DIA opened, bondholders filed charges claiming they had been misled. If they had known about the problems, the bondholders asserted, they never would have invested in the airport in the first place. The bondholders feared they would lose money because problems with the DIA would result in lower interest earnings on the bonds.

Minority firms targeted

Other investigations were concerned with the awarding of contracts to minority-owned firms. One of the local businesses that gave Pena money at the beginning of the project was Alvarado Construction Incorporated, a business owned by Robert and Linda Alvarado. As a result of the couple's support, their company was awarded a contract to build an airport office building. Alvarado Construction ended up making $23 million for the job instead of the budgeted $13 million (one of the largest cost overruns). As a result of this overrun and reports of shoddy workmanship in the building itself, the company's construction practices came under close scrutiny. A more serious charge was that unsafe procedures on the part of Alvarado Construction led to the deaths of two workers in a construction accident. Investigators ultimately found that the accident resulted from human error.

In another investigation, the FBI looked into a claim made by a contractor (a businessman hired to provide certain major construction services) named Steve Chaves, who owned a company called CSI Trucking. Chaves claimed that the cement used in runway construction was too thin. When cracks in the runways developed, they were quickly patched with thicker cement or glue before the DIA opened.

A successful misadventure?

In spite its troubled history, the DIA had a good record during its first year of business. In 1996 the Federal Aviation Administration (FAA) reported that the DIA was one of the best airports in the country. It had very few flight delays, and people enjoyed using the terminal (the building that houses such facilities as ticket counters, boarding gates, shops, and restaurants). Furthermore, the airport reported a yearly profit of $8 million, which helped to defray its enormous construction and operating costs. In addition, the DIA had a truly great design.

Passengers wait for their flight at Denver International Airport. First approved in 1984, the airport finally opened for operation in 1995.

The three-story terminal featured thirty-four white towers resembling the Rocky Mountains, which surrounded the facility in the background. A $7.5 million art collection was displayed in the terminals, which also contained many exclusive stores and shops.

The DIA was also praised for the functional layout of its runways (areas outside the airport where planes takeoff and land). The five runways fanned out like a pinwheel, permitting air traffic controllers to shift traffic in any direction according to wind patterns. (This was important because snowstorms occur frequently in Denver during the winter.) The new airport also had the most effective and environmentally safe deicing (ice removal) facilities available anywhere. This was crucial because of Denver's cold winters and the chronic problem of crashes resulting from ice buildup on airplane wings.

In addition to being the first American airport built in two decades, the DIA was also the first major flight facility designed to be environmentally conscious. The Environmental Protection Agency worked with designers to minimize pollution in many areas of the airport. For example, all of the vehicles at the airport ran on natural gas. Designers also created the Automated Guideway Transit System (AGTS), a train that transported passengers around the terminal. Since the train was electric, it released no toxic (poisonous) fumes.

Only time will tell

Even though travelers might have to drive out of their way to get to the DIA, on a grander scale the airport is well situated. It is located midway between two new airports in Europe and Asia—one in Munich, Germany, and the other in Japan. This location advantage could eventually make Colorado a center for international commerce. The DIA is already the ninth largest airport in the world, and it has the capacity to expand into the largest by the year 2020.

The DIA's major drawback continues to be its enormous cost, a debt that is far from being paid off. Operating expenditures are more than two times higher than those at Stapleton, the old airport. Critics of the project still believe that the DIA proves it is unwise to embark on publicly funded ventures that lead officials to misguide investors and increase the burden on taxpayers; they also worry that cost-cutting measures may have influenced the quality of the final product. Other observers—despite some misgivings—are still willing to wait and see if the airport turns out to be a long-term success.

FOR FURTHER REFERENCE

Books

Hedges, Stephen J., Brian Duffy, and Ancel Martinez. "A Taj Mahal in the Rockies: The Bizarre Story of Denver's New Airport—and It Isn't Over Yet." *U.S. News & World Report.* February 13, 1995.

Kaufman-Rosen, Leslie. "Finally! It's Here!" *Newsweek.* March 6, 1995.

The Aldrich Ames Spy Case

1985 TO 1994

Aldrich Ames managed to rise quickly in the CIA ranks, even though his superiors warned that he should not be entrusted with any significant responsibilities.

Aldrich Ames committed the most damaging act of betrayal in the history of the U.S. Central Intelligence Agency (CIA). Ames had worked for the CIA since he was a teenager, and in 1967 he became a spy against the Soviet Union. In the mid-1980s, however, Ames turned on his own colleagues and became a mole (a spy for the Soviet Union) within the CIA. Ames revealed hundreds of American intelligence operations to the KGB, the Soviet counterpart to the CIA. Ames's actions also caused the deaths of ten Soviet spies who were working for the United States. Ames engaged in treason primarily for money, but he also thought that the spying game played by the United States and the Soviet Union was meaningless. In fact, during his trial Ames expressed deep contempt for CIA espionage activities. Ames's actions—and the long-term damage they caused—are doubly troubling because his CIA employers had continued to promote him long after he should have been fired.

An incompetent spy

Ames managed to rise quickly in the CIA ranks, even though his superiors warned that he should not be entrusted with any significant responsibilities. After Ames completed his college degree in 1967, he entered the training program for CIA case officers and learned all the tricks of the spy craft. For his first assignment he was sent to Ankara, the capital of Turkey, and a hotbed of espionage (spying) activity. As a spy, Ames was a flop. His station chief (supervisor) found him to be lazy, and this judgment nearly led Ames to quit the CIA. But he decided to stay with the agency and returned to the United States.

Ames was then appointed to the Soviet division of the CIA's Directorate of Operations and learned the Russian language. At this point he began drinking heavily and frequently became distracted. For instance, in 1975 he was sent on a mission to deliver some documents to a Soviet informer, but he left the briefcase containing the important papers on a New York City subway. Luckily for Ames, someone turned the briefcase over to the Federal Bureau of Investigation (FBI; the FBI is the federal government agency responsible for investigating criminal activity within the United States).

During the next five years Ames worked in the United States and several other countries while receiving numerous promotions. A dark period in his life began when he was sent to Mexico City, where he spent most of his time drinking and sleeping instead of spying. In Mexico City Ames met Maria del Rosario Casas Dupuy, a Colombian cultural officer. The two were married, and Ames was reassigned to CIA headquarters at Langley, Virginia. Although the Mexico City station chief had requested that Ames receive treatment for alcoholism, this advice was not heeded by top officials. The CIA's personnel and security offices had also warned that Ames should not be assigned to sensitive posts, but again, no one gave serious attention to the recommendation. On the contrary, Ames was promoted to the position of chief of counterintelligence (blocking an enemy's sources of information) at the CIA's Soviet Division.

Has contempt for spy game

After the Ameses were married they acquired expensive tastes that could not be supported on a CIA salary. Around this time Ames also began to seethe with anger at the two most powerful countries in the world—the United States and the Soviet Union—for squandering their energies on the spying game. In his view the game was ridiculous: Spies would recruit spies, who in turn would recruit other spies, then those spies would recruit others, in an endless circle.

ALDRICH AMES Aldrich Hazen Ames (1941–) was born in River Falls, Wisconsin. His father, Carleton Cecil Ames, was a professor of European and Asian history. His mother, Rachel Aldrich Ames, was a high school English teacher. In 1953 Carleton Ames was recruited by the CIA and assigned to Rangoon, Burma. His job was to recruit agents, gather intelligence on political leaders, and watch Russian and Chinese activities. An alcoholic and a failure, he returned to the United States after only two years abroad. At age sixteen Aldrich, who was known as Rick, began working at the CIA. After graduating from high school, he briefly attended the University of Chicago. In a short time, he returned to the CIA. Without a college education, however, Ames could not become a spy. He finally earned his college degree in 1967. As his actions later revealed, Ames proved to have the perfect personality for spy work, including a stunning ability to tell lies.

Ames soon realized that he was in an advantageous position. His new job gave him an opportunity to make a considerable amount of money by exploiting both sides. Ames had the names of two Russians who had approached the CIA and offered to become spies for the United States against the Soviet Union. The CIA turned the Russians down, knowing they were really double agents (spies who worked for the Soviet Union while pretending to spy for the United States). Ames knew the Soviets were not aware that the CIA had found out the agents were liars. In April 1985 he gave this information to the Soviet embassy in Washington, D.C. In return, Soviet diplomat Sergei Chuvakhin gave Ames a package. It contained five hundred new one hundred dollar bills.

Steals CIA documents

All of a sudden, Ames was struck by the seriousness of his act. He could be found out, so he had to protect himself. The best way was to reveal the names of Soviet agents who were working for the CIA. Ames also saw this as a chance to make even more money, especially since the Soviets had paid $50,000 for useless information about spies the CIA had not even hired. Ames started assembling documents that would be valuable to the Soviets, including the names of Soviet agents working for the United States and its allies. On June 13, 1985, Ames left his office carrying CIA papers in plastic bags inside his briefcase. Never before had so many documents been smuggled out of CIA headquarters. Ames did not have to worry about being caught, however, because the CIA no longer checked the briefcases of employees as they left the building.

On the day of his second meeting with Chuvakhin, Ames simply put the documents in a shopping bag and drove to the rendezvous at a local restaurant. The two men dined while the open shopping bag was tucked under the table. Chuvakhin was pleased with Ames's information, and he promised that two million dollars had been set aside in payment. The money would be issued in installments of $25,000 a month.

Indulges expensive tastes

In the fall of 1985, Ames received another promotion. This time he was named chief at the CIA bureau in Rome, Italy. Ames was once again dealing with the Soviet Union. While he was stationed in Rome for the next three years, he continued to smuggle documents to his Soviet contact. With a million dollars now tucked away in a Swiss bank, Ames started buying expensive Italian suits. His fellow employees noticed the change in his appearance, but they did not give it any further thought.

In spite of his improved fashion image, Ames was still drinking heavily. Once he flew to Zurich, Switzerland, to meet his Soviet contact when the meeting was supposed to be held in Vienna, Austria. At a Fourth of July picnic he was boisterous and rude to a guest. After Ames left the party he passed out on the street and the police took him to a hospital. Yet no one at the CIA seemed to care how badly Ames behaved. On his return to the United States in 1989, he was promoted to chief of the Western Europe branch of the Soviet Division. Ames was now free to indulge his expensive tastes. He bought a $540,000 home and a new Jaguar sportscar. Ames's CIA superiors wondered about their agent's newfound wealth, but their investigations indicated that the money came from Maria Ames's family.

Spies disappear

In the meantime, the Soviet Union was acting on the information provided by its new spy. From the fall of 1985 until early 1986, the KGB rounded up the men whose names Ames had supplied. KGB officials killed ten of the men and imprisoned the others. Soon officials at CIA headquarters became alarmed: twenty top Soviet spies had disappeared. This development could not be the result of spy-craft mistakes the spies themselves had made. Everything pointed to a mole, a traitor within the ranks of the CIA. Nevertheless, senior officers would not admit to the possibility of a spy working in their midst. They preferred to blame operational errors, so no major investigation was launched. But Clair George, deputy director of operations, thought something should be done. He authorized a secret task force to look into the disappearances of the spies.

Secret task force formed

Jeanne Vertefeuille, a career CIA employee, was appointed head of the task force. Serving with her were Fran Smith, Sandy Grimes, and two retirees, Benjamin Franklin Pepper and Daniel Niesciur. The investigation would prove to be difficult. The investigators' job was to look at the cases and ask these questions: Which CIA offices handled the files? Who knew about them? Which officers had access to the files? Was there any pattern? The group's task was immediately complicated by the KGB. The Soviet spy agency knew that the CIA was searching for a mole, so they tried to throw the investigation off track by sending out people who gave false information. One of these people was Edward Lee Howard, a CIA traitor who had defected (left because of a change in ideology) to the Soviet Union in 1986. Howard revealed several "secrets" to the CIA, but the task force found they were all lies.

The tactic worked. Task force efforts were delayed for years. A break finally came in November 1989. A female CIA employee supplied a number of facts to Dan Payne, an investigator with the task force. The employee revealed that Ames had purchased a new house, had spent money beyond his means, and had access to files on the missing spies. Also, contrary to previous CIA findings, Ames's wife was not from a wealthy family. Payne eventually learned that Ames had paid cash for his home and had made large cash transactions at banks. Inexplicably, Payne was pulled off the case and reassigned. On December 5, 1990, Payne sent a memorandum to the CIA security office arguing that there was enough evidence to justify an investigation of Ames.

Efforts intensified

Early in 1991 Paul Redmond was appointed deputy chief of the CIA counterintelligence center. He had disliked Ames for many years, so he was highly interested in Payne's information. Redmond and Vertefeuille made an appointment with Raymond Mislock Jr., head the Soviet section of the intelligence division, and Robert Wade, assistant section chief. The four investigators decided to launch a joint investigation to find the traitor. While these plans were under way, however, Ames was given yet another vote of confidence by the CIA. In August

1991, the head of the KGB tried to replace Soviet premier Mikhail Gorbachev (1931–) during an unsuccessful coup (overthrow of the government) in Moscow. The Soviet spy service had now been placed in its most vulnerable position ever. The CIA needed a countermove to topple its arch enemy, so Ames was put in charge of a task force to eliminate the KGB. At the time no one was aware of the grim irony in this situation.

Within two years the investigative trail was leading to Ames. Finally CIA officials called Ames in for an interview and asked how the names of the missing spies could have been discovered by the Soviets. Ames concocted a story about foolishly leaving a safe open and suggested that a mole within the CIA had taken the spies' files from the safe. The investigators thought otherwise, however, and focused their scrutiny even more directly on Ames.

By now Payne was back on the task force. When he took a closer look at Ames's finances he discovered the agent was spending $30,000 a month with credit cards. Wire transfers totaling one million dollars had been deposited into his banking account, while Ames himself had deposited $500,000 in cash. Task force member Sandy Grimes, who had also been doing some digging, found the most crucial evidence. He compared the dates of Ames's meetings with Chuvakhin with the dates of his bank deposits in 1985 and 1986. Grimes discovered that the deposits were made shortly after the meetings. CIA investigators now believed that Ames was the traitor, and they turned their findings over to the FBI.

FBI launches Nightmover

On May 12, 1993, the FBI opened its case, which was code named "Nightmover." A nine-man surveillance team was assigned to follow Ames and his wife. (Eventually more than 100 special agents were used to make the case against Ames.) Each member of the team had a special function, such as electronic surveillance or computer information retrieval. Agents disguised themselves as homeless men and garbage collectors so it would be easier to follow Ames. On July 20, 1993, Ames parked his car outside the J. Edgar Hoover Building in Washington, D.C. While he was gone, a special Technical Services Squad commandeered the car. In a matter of minutes the squad had planted a tiny electronic device that would enable them to track Ames. The squad then got approval for a ninety-day wiretap on Ames's telephone through the Foreign Intelligence Surveillance Act.

The first break in the case came on September 8: An intercepted phone message led to the location of the site where Ames left messages for the Russians. Agents next searched Ames's trash and found a note saying: "I am ready to meet at B[ogata] Oct." The note gave U.S. Attorney General Janet Reno (1938–) grounds for authorizing entry into the Ameses' home.

Incriminating evidence found

During the night of October 9, while Ames and his wife were on vacation, agents slipped into the couple's house. The most incriminating evidence came from Ames's home computer, which contained a complete record of his espionage activities, as well as highly classified CIA documents. In November, the agents followed Ames to Bogotá, Colombia. Traveling under tourist visas and using their own names, the agents staked out a number of locations with video cameras. Ames eluded detection, however, and returned to the United States with $125,000.

Aldrich Ames after his arrest in 1994. Ames's treasonous activities led to the deaths of ten Soviet spies working for the United States government.

The FBI finally decided to catch Ames in the act of treason (the betrayal of one's country). Agents placed a video camera in a tree across from Ames's home, but it turned up nothing. By this time the team was getting nervous. The longer the investigation dragged on, the greater the likelihood that Ames would find out about it. They decided on another strategy. Ames would soon be taking a trip Moscow on CIA business. To keep him in the United States, the FBI scheduled a National Security Council briefing on drug trafficking at the White House. FBI officials invited Ames to be the guest speaker.

Traitor goes to prison

Ames rescheduled his Moscow trip for February 22, 1994. The Nightmover team decided it was time to act. They planned to arrest Ames on February 21, which was President's Day and a federal holiday. A CIA official phoned Ames at home, telling him he was needed at work. As Ames drove away from his home in his Jaguar, he encountered an FBI roadblock a few blocks away. Cars converged on the Jaguar from all sides. Minutes later Ames found himself handcuffed in the backseat of an unmarked government car as an FBI agent informed him he was under arrest. Maria Ames was also arrested, and both were charged with espionage. Little more than a month later, on April 28, 1994, Ames received a life sentence. His wife was sentenced to five years. Ames used the convictions as a platform for denouncing the CIA. After he had gone to prison he gave a nationally televised interview in which he called spying an insignificant and irrelevant activity.

FOR FURTHER REFERENCE

Books

Weiner, Tim, David Johnston and Neil A. Lewis. *Betrayal: The Story of Alrich Ames, An American Spy.* New York City: Random House, 1995.

Periodicals

Wise, David. "Ames Spy Hunt." *Time.* May 22, 1995, pp. 55–61.

The Fall of John Gotti

1990 TO 1992

Mafia boss John Gotti violated the mob code by becoming a celebrity.

From 1985 to 1991, John Gotti was the boss of the Gambino crime family, one of the largest Mafia organizations in America. During his violent career, Gotti earned the nickname "Teflon Don." No criminal charges would ever stick to this slippery man: Every time the mob leader went to court, all he had to do was bribe a juror and he was off the hook. But Bruce Muow, the leader of the Federal Bureau of Investigation (FBI) C-16 Organized Crime Squad, vowed to put a stop to Gotti's activities. In 1987 Muow met with his top agents and together they vowed to put the Gambino family out of business forever. Over the next five years, the FBI squad mounted a daring and spectacular surveillance project that brought down organized crime in New York City. Gotti had too much confidence in the Mafia system of loyalty to expect that his own underboss, Salvatore Gravano, would turn on him. What resulted from the FBI's intervention surprised not only Gotti, but the entire world.

FBI plants microphone

In 1988 the FBI began planting microphones inside Gotti's headquarters, the Ravenite Social Club in Manhattan (a part of New York City). Based on intelligence provided by informants (people who provide information, usually for money), Gotti held meetings with his men at a table inside the Ravenite. Supposedly, all the C-16 squad had to do was plant a microphone near this table and they would be able to monitor Gotti's conversations.

On a cold night in February, FBI agent John Kravec set out to plant a microphone inside the Ravenite. He was dropped off behind the club in a refrigerator box, from which he picked the lock to the back door of the building. Once inside, Kravec planted a microphone in a heating duct that was located near Gotti's table. Fortunately, this part of the mission was a success. When Muow listened to the tapes, however, he was disappointed to find that all of the voices were drowned out when the heat came on in the building. The C-16 squad needed a new strategy.

Agents spy on mob

Another problem arose: When a microphone finally did pick up voices, the FBI could not tell who was talking. Therefore, the C-16 squad had to set up an observation point where they could monitor who went in and out of Gotti's headquarters. If a new voice came on the tape, the FBI could surmise that it was the same man who had just walked into the club. In April of 1988, agent George Gabriel found an apartment across the street from the Ravenite with a view of the front door to the club. The C-16 squad proceeded to set up binoculars, video cameras, and tape recorders inside their hideout. Luckily, the agents got excellent pictures of mob members circulating through the front door of the Ravenite. However, because they were still relying on the same audio microphone, the agents were unable to record enough conversations. Muow realized he was going to have to place a microphone at a different site.

FBI gets first clue

One year after the C-16 squad set up their observation point, they received their first clue as to the location of Gotti's real meeting place. On April 26, 1989, Mafia man Tommy Gambino was arrested. As soon as he posted bail (a sum of money paid for temporary release from jail), he rushed to the Ravenite for a meeting with Gotti. Video surveillance showed Gambino entering the front door of the Ravenite, but not leaving. From this and other data, Muow deduced that Gambino went with Gotti out the back door of the club and up the stairs

THE MAFIA The Mafia originated in Italy during the feudal period of the Middle Ages (c. 500–c. 1600; feudalism was a land-based system of strict social structure headed by the aristocracy). Mafia members were brigands (bandits) from Sicily who were hired by lords (heads of the aristocracy) to guard their estates. In exchange, the Mafia was given protection from local legal authorities. Out of this arrangement grew the Mafia belief that the law was of no value and that justice had to be achieved independently. Mafia members formed small groups known as families, which were often in competition with one another.

The Mafia was gradually established in the United States (where it was often known as "The Black Hand") during extensive Italian immigration in the nineteenth and twentieth centuries. The Mafia organization, sometimes referred to as the "Cosa Nostra," consisted of several families. These families competed for control of illegal operations such as gambling, narcotics, prostitution, and labor union rackets in most major American cities. By the mid-twentieth century the Mafia was also involved in police corruption, money laundering (concealing illegal funds through legal channels), the trucking industry, and construction trades. For most of the century federal authorities tried unsuccessfully to break up the mob. The conviction of John Gotti and the subsequent fall of the Gambino family in 1992 finally damaged the power of the Mafia in the United States.

The Mafia has been the subject of numerous feature films and documentaries. The best-known Hollywood movies are *The Godfather* (1972), *The Godfather, Part 2* (1974), and *The Godfather, Part 3* (1990). The first two parts of the fictional saga of the Corleone family won several Academy Awards. In 1998 the American Broadcasting Company (ABC-TV) presented *Witness to the Mob,* an adaptation of Sammy the Bull Gravano's autobiography, *Underboss* (1997). The Arts and Entertainment (A&E) cable television network also aired a documentary on the Mafia titled *American Justice* in 1998.

to an apartment above the Ravenite. When Gambino left, he simply went out the back door of the building. Finally, on November 21, 1989, Kravec placed a microphone in the stairwell behind the Ravenite. He put another listening device in the apartment of the widow of a deceased Mafia member, Michael Cirelli. Kravec planted it in a videocassette recorder in the living room of the apartment. This time, he was successful.

C-16 gets evidence

The FBI received its first transmission from the Cirelli apartment on the evening of November 30, 1989. The agents recorded a conversation between Gotti, Salvatore Gravano, Frank

John Gotti (second from right) headed the powerful Gambino Mafia family. Gotti's arrest in 1990 helped to diminish the power of the Mafia, especially in New York City.

Locascio, and Michael Coiro. Gravano (also called "Sammy the Bull") was Gotti's *consigliere* (an Italian word for Mafia adviser) at the time. Locascio (also called "Frankie Lo") was the acting underboss (second in command to Gotti), and Coiro was a Mafia attorney. At last the C-16 squad had found Gotti's meeting place. The most important transmission, however, came later, on December 12, 1989. During this conversation, Gotti complained to Frankie Lo that Sammy the Bull was gaining too much power.

Gotti's statements were unusual because he and Gravano, who seemed to be a loyal pair, were the backbone of the entire Gambino family operation. Along with this incriminating evidence, the FBI overheard information regarding the structure of the Gambino family, murder conspiracies, labor racketeering, and communication with other Cosa Nostra families. The FBI finally had enough evidence to arrest the "Teflon Don." (A don is a powerful Mafia leader.)

The Fall of John Gotti | 687

Gotti arrested

Audio surveillance was shut down on June 22, 1990, after the FBI had spent more than $1 million on the project. Video surveillance, on the other hand, remained in operation. Finally, on December 11, 1990, the FBI was prepared to arrest Gotti. That evening, the C-16 squad watched from their observation post while the Mafia boss and his top men entered the Ravenite. As soon as the men were all inside, agent Gabriel and his men stormed the club. Even though the Ravenite was full of Gambino capos (leaders), the FBI had warrants to arrest only three men. In addition to Gotti, Gabriel arrested Sammy the Bull, who was now the underboss, and Frankie Lo, who had been promoted to consigliere. After ordering the rest of the men in the room to stay calm, Gotti surrendered without a fight. To him, the fuss was routine.

Gotti betrays Gravano

By December 14, the three Mafia leaders were in court listening to their own voices on the FBI surveillance tapes. When Sammy the Bull heard the conversation from December 12, 1989, he was absolutely furious. He could not understand why Gotti would talk so badly about him behind his back. Gravano, a forty-four-year-old millionaire construction executive and the father of two children, had built his life around the Gambino family. Now he faced the possibility of spending the rest of his days in prison along with Gotti and Locascio. Gravano was so angered by Gotti's betrayal that he decided to make a deal with the FBI.

Gravano's disillusionment with Gotti had actually begun long before he heard the tape. Gotti took great pleasure in outsmarting the law, so when he managed to elude prosecution in the court trials he thought he was infallible. He began courting the press, and soon he had scores of fans—Gotti called them his "public"—who followed him along the streets of New York City. Gotti also brought attention to himself by sporting expensive clothes and encouraging his other nickname, "Dapper Don." Gravano become increasingly uncomfortable with Gotti's need to be a celebrity. In Gravano's mind, this behavior directly violated the Mafia "code" that a don must remain anonymous. By bringing attention to himself, a don invites unwanted scrutiny of the Mafia.

Starting on March 2, 1992, Gravano spent six days in court testifying against Gotti. He told the prosecutors everything, including how Gotti became the boss and how the Gambino family operation worked. He also gave a full account of the murder of Paul Castellano (former head of the Gambino family). Finally, on April 2, 1992, Gotti and Locascio were found guilty on fourteen counts, including the murder of Castellano. Gravano was not prosecuted.

Gravano goes free

The FBI is accustomed to using informants to solve crimes. They never expected, however, one of their best informants to be Sammy the Bull. Gravano told the agents absolutely everything they needed to know. After Gotti was convicted, Gravano testified in four more trials that led to the conviction of thirty-seven other criminals. He turned from being one of the Mafia's biggest players into its worst enemy. Never before had an informant made such a giant leap. In 1994, Gravano was rewarded for his testimony by being required to serve only five years in prison (he actually served only three years). This was a very light sentence considering the fact that he had been involved in nineteen murders (eleven of which were sanctioned by Gotti).

Mob brought down

In the end, Gravano blamed all of the crimes on Gotti; he also held Gotti responsible for destroying the Mafia. Gravano claimed that Gotti had turned the Mafia system of loyalty into a fraud, and he knew that it would have been only a matter of time before he himself was killed by Gotti. Gotti eventually began serving a life sentence without parole at the maximum security prison in Marion, Illinois. The trial of his son, John Gotti, Jr.—also a prominent Mafia figure—began in 1997. Gravano is out of the FBI's Witness Protection Program, and still doing business. In 1997, however, the families of Gravano's murder victims filed lawsuits against him. By 1998 newspapers were reporting that the Mafia had been virtually eliminated in

New York City. The fall of Gotti and the Gambino family was largely responsible for this historic development.

FOR FURTHER REFERENCE

Books

Maas, Peter. *Underboss: Sammy the Bull Gravano's Story of Life in the Mafia.* New York City: HarperCollins, 1997.

The Sinking of the *Andrea Gail*

OCTOBER 28, 1991

On October 28, 1991, the *Andrea Gail,* a commercial swordfishing boat from Gloucester, Massachusetts, was lost in a storm off the coast of Nova Scotia, Canada. The captain of the boat, Frank "Billy" Tyne, and his four-man crew all drowned during the squall. The storm was a mighty "Nor'easter," one of the worst squalls of the century. ("Nor'easter" is the pronunciation used by fishermen on the eastern coast of the United States for the term "Northeaster," a storm with winds out of the northeast.) Weather conditions were so terrible because the Nor'easter collided with Hurricane Grace, causing what meteorologists call "the perfect storm." Ultimately, the crew of the *Andrea Gail* died because they wanted to get one last, big catch of the year—no matter what the danger. Ironically, the ship's high-tech devices were of little use to the crew during the storm. Working in a profession that has not essentially changed in over three hundred years, the fishermen aboard the *Andrea Gail* simply fell prey to the strength of natural forces, the same forces that plagued their fishing ancestors.

Fishermen live with danger all the time, so it is no surprise that the *Andrea Gail*'s crew was brave enough to face "the perfect storm."

Crewmen sense danger

The *Andrea Gail* was a sound boat. It was seventy-feet long, and its hull was made of one continuously welded steel plate. Made in Panama City (capital of the Republic of Panama, on

691

CANADA

QUEBEC

ONTARIO

Lake Ontario

NEW YORK

PENNSYLVANIA

VT.

N.H.

MASS.

CONN.

R.I.

MD.

N.J.

DEL.

VA.

MAINE

NEW BRUNSWICK

PRINCE EDWARD I.

Cape Breton Island

NOVA SCOTIA

Gloucester

Governor's Island

ATLANTIC OCEAN

On October 28, 1991, four days into the return trip home, the *Andrea Gail* is lost in "the perfect storm." The crew, the boat, and all of its cargo were never recovered.

Captain Frank "Billy" Tyne and his three-man crew set out from Gloucester on September 23, 1991, on a month-long fishing expedition aboard the *Andrea Gail.*

0   100   200 mi
0   160   320 km

The crew of the *Andrea Gail* fishing boat was willing to risk severe weather conditions in order to catch one last, lucrative haul of swordfish.

the Panama Canal), the boat was considered to be top of the line. Even a vessel as solid as the *Andrea Gail,* however, could not stand up against a huge storm. In a Nor'easter, waves can top 100 feet; in fact, the sea spray alone is enough to drown a person. This is the kind of storm that swept the *Andrea Gail* away on that fateful day in 1991.

Captain Tyne originally had a difficult time rounding up a crew for his fall fishing expedition. This was Tyne's second trip on the *Andrea Gail,* and he evidently believed that the ship could endure almost anything. Other fishermen disagreed. For instance, Doug Cosco, who had gone on a previous fishing expedition with Tyne, walked off the *Andrea Gail* simply because he had a bad feeling about the upcoming trip. Another fisherman named Adam Randall backed out because he was also apprehensive about the journey. Tyne finally convinced

Gloucester natives David "Sully" Sullivan and Robert Shatford to be his crewmen. He also hired Alfred Pierre, a Jamaican from New York City whose family lived in Portland, Maine, and Dale "Murph" Murphy.

Andrea Gail lost

Having finally assembled a crew, Tyne set out from Gloucester on September 23, 1991. During the month-long expedition, the Andrea Gail took in almost fifteen tons of swordfish. If he had made it home, Tyne would have made almost $20,000, and his crew $4,500 to $6,500 each. After turning around to come home on October 24, the Andrea Gail was lost at 6:00 P.M. on October 28. The boat was officially reported missing two days later. The U.S. Coast Guard at Governor's Island, New York, immediately launched a search for the Andrea Gail, but finally gave up ten days later, on November 8. The only evidence of the boat the Coast Guard ever found were a few fuel drums. Everything else, including the boat's payload (the swordfish) and crew, was completely lost.

One mysterious aspect of the Andrea Gail accident was that there was no distress call from the boat. All fishing boats are equipped with an Emergency Position Indicating Radio Beacon (EPIRB). This device is usually turned on so that when a boat sinks, a radio signal is transmitted via satellite to the shore. For some reason, the EPIRB on the Andrea Gail was turned off, and no one knows why.

Danger a part of the job

To say that East Coast fishermen are merely overconfident thrill seekers is inaccurate. Fishermen need to make a living like everyone else, and danger is just an incidental part of the job. Tyne probably should have backed out when he had a difficult time finding a crew. His expedition took place late in the season (a time when winter storms are forming at sea), and the apprehension of the other fishermen should have been a sign that foul weather was approaching. However, the great money-making potential of the trip probably outweighed any other priority in Tyne's mind. The fact that the EPIRB beacon had been turned off on the Andrea Gail is mysterious, and might even suggest foul play. But in the end, "the perfect storm" accident can be considered a misadventure that resulted from over-confidence. Unfortunately, it was the kind of overconfidence that is necessary for fishermen to make a living from the sea.

No stranger to adventure

The Perfect Storm (1997) is a best-selling novel about the *Andrea Gail* accident of 1991. The book's author, Sebastian Junger, is himself a thrill seeker who knows what it means to have a dangerous job. In 1984 he received a degree in cultural anthropology (the study of human societies) from Wesleyan University in Middleton, Connecticut. Afterward he started writing fiction, but ended up working construction and waiting tables. Then Junger published articles in major magazines such as *Outside*. When he worked as a stringer (free-lance reporter) for the Associated Press doing radio reports, his life became even more exciting. Finally, Junger discovered the dangerous and well-paying job of tree cutting. Junger sometimes had to climb 100-foot trees with a heavy chainsaw. He has had accidents in the trees and has the stitches to prove it.

Because of Junger's experience with dangerous jobs, he understood the fishermen's love for the danger and excitement of the sea. *The Perfect Storm* includes many anecdotes about accidents that are a part of a fisherman's everyday life. For instance, Dale Murphy once got hooked in the hand by a fishing line that pulled him off the boat. Another time, a mako shark clamped onto Murphy's arm, and his friends had to beat the shark to death. Murphy even collided with a British nuclear submarine that tore a hole in his boat. Considering that fishermen live with danger all the time, it is no surprise that *Andrea Gail's* crew was brave enough to face "the perfect storm."

FOR FURTHER REFERENCE

Books

Junger, Sebastian. *The Perfect Storm: A True Story of Men Against the Sea.* New York City: Norton, 1997.

The Assault on Ice Skater Nancy Kerrigan

JANUARY 6, 1994

The attack on ice skater Nancy Kerrigan destroyed Tonya Harding's dreams of fame and financial security.

Tonya Harding had always been the exception to the rule in the world of women's figure skating. A tough, unpolished young woman, she presented a sharp contrast to the traditional, graceful image of female figure skaters. Yet Harding's performances often impressed even her staunchest critics. From the age of four, she pursued the sport with intense energy and determination. Her tumultuous career was marked by two recurring themes: an abundance of ability and a lack of funds. Harding's personal life was also problematic, beginning with an abusive childhood, followed in later years by a troubled marriage. It was Harding's relationship with her former husband, Jeff Gillooly, that led to the event which ended the skater's chances of becoming an Olympic champion. On January 6, 1994, Harding's foremost rival, Nancy Kerrigan (1969–), was assaulted during a practice session for a national skating competition. A whirlwind of accusations soon began circulating in the media, charging Harding and Gillooly with direct involvement in the attack. Gillooly and several of his associates were ultimately found guilty. Although Harding herself was never implicated in the crime, many people still believed she had played a role in trying to eliminate Kerrigan as an Olympic rival.

Shows great potential

From the time Harding first put on skates, she showed great potential on the ice. Diane Rawlinson became Harding's coach and remained with the skater for most of her career. When Harding was only five years old, Rawlinson predicted that she could become an Olympic champion. At the age of nine, Harding executed her first triple jump on a dare. After twelve years of skating, she won her first title, at the Northwest Pacific championships—a finish that thrust her into the national spotlight. A year later, when Harding was sixteen, her parents removed her from high school midway through her sophomore year to insure her continued success. (Harding later received a high school graduation equivalency degree [GED] from a local community college.) By 1989 Harding had risen high in the ranks of potential skating stars. After winning a third-place finish in the national championships and victories in two international events, she became a strong contender for the 1992 Olympic team. With the gold medal and huge earnings constantly on her mind, Harding was rising to the top.

Tonya Harding's physical skating style contrasted sharply with that of her main rival, skater Nancy Kerrigan.

Troubled marriage, successful career

While Harding's career was blossoming, she fell in love with Gillooly. The couple was married—without Lavona and Al Harding's approval—on March 18, 1990, in Vancouver, Washington. Harding was nineteen and Gillooly was twenty-two. Fifteen months later, Harding filed for divorce and sought a restraining order from the court to keep Gillooly away from her. (A restraining order is a legal document that restricts access between people. Violating a restraining order can lead to a fine or jail time.) Harding claimed Gillooly had verbally and physically assaulted her. Despite the volatile state of her personal life, however, Harding flourished on the ice. In 1991 her achievements included the national seniors title, second place at the

TONYA HARDING Tonya Harding (1970–) was born in Portland, Oregon, the daughter of Lavona and Al Harding. She was raised in modest surroundings where lack of money was a constant issue. Harding's father drove a truck and her mother was a waitress. Throughout her childhood, Harding lived in eight different houses in six different communities. She began skating at the age of three and a half. Given the Harding family's limited budget, the cost of skating equipment and rink fees were staggering. In fact, Harding's father was not able to afford the fees at the rink where Harding practiced and where a banner now hangs in her honor.

Harding once recalled that, to earn money, she and her mother collected bottles and cans along the highway and turned them in for refunds. The skater remembered that this motherly show of support was an unusual event. While Lavona Harding made many of her daughter's costumes and was constantly present at her practices, she was also sharp to criticize and physically abusive. By her own account, Harding had a much warmer relationship with her father, who taught his daughter how to break down a car engine, hunt, fish, and shoot pool.

world championships, and a victory in Skate America, an annual international event held in the United States. With her combative, storming style, Harding was making a name for herself in a world where a person of her demeanor usually did not fit in.

In 1992 Harding was reunited with Gillooly. The reconciliation did not help Harding's skating career. She slipped to third place in the national championships and finished a disappointing fourth at the 1992 Winter Olympic Games in Albertville, France. Her ranking also fell at the 1993 U.S. Nationals, where she finished in fourth place. In July 1993 a frustrated Harding was again seeking a divorce and restraining order, once again citing physical abuse. After the divorce, a third attempt at reconciliation with Gillooly lasted until the incident with Kerrigan.

Assault on Nancy Kerrigan

On January 6, 1994, Nancy Kerrigan was getting ready to practice for the U.S. Figure Skating Championships in Detroit, Michigan. As she approached the practice rink at Cobo Hall, a man dressed in black ran toward her. Using a swift motion he struck Kerrigan's right knee with a collapsible metal baton, then darted out of the building. The shocking incident left Kerrigan asking, "Why me?" The resulting investigation led to

TWO DIFFERENT WORLDS

The attack on Nancy Kerrigan brought into sharp focus one of the reasons Tonya Harding never fit well into the figure skating world. The two skaters were very different people, both in their lifestyles and their approach to skating. For example, Kerrigan's manner was sincere and unassuming, and she had a coolly elegant style on the ice. Harding, on the other hand, had a tough demeanor and she skated with raw—and visibly physical—power.

Although Kerrigan was injured in the assault, she was able to regain her strength and win a silver medal at the 1994 Winter Olympic Games. Kerrigan's comeback was largely due to her stable family life and upbringing. Kerrigan had always received unconditional love from her parents and her extended family, who supported her at competitions. In sharp contrast, Harding's life was extremely unstable. Her parents were divorced and her mother, who was married six times, was known to be abusive. While Kerrigan was sheltered in her family's home after the assault, Harding was thrust into the spotlight. Kerrigan later received major product endorsements and television and book deals.

Harding and her entourage. Harding's denial of any role in the attack was put under close scrutiny from the start, while physical evidence led to the circle of people who served as Harding's support team. Eventually investigators learned that one of three men had attacked Kerrigan in order to take her out of the national competition and dash her hopes of going to the 1994 Winter Olympic Games in Lillehammer, Norway.

Bodyguard admits guilt

In the months leading up to the assault, Harding had once again fallen upon hard times. She was increasingly desperate for money and had lost Rawlinson, her manager (and last hope for product endorsement contracts). Perhaps most significantly, Harding hired a bodyguard named Shawn Eckardt. Eckardt had a criminal record and was eventually arrested for his involvement in the Kerrigan attack. In fact, the break in the Kerrigan case came after Eckardt's admission of guilt to a fellow classmate in a legal procedure class at Pioneer Pacific College in Portland, Oregon. Eckardt freely spoke of the Kerrigan plan in front of Eugene Saunders, a young pastor. Disturbed by the story, Saunders passed the information along to Gary Crowe, a private detective who was also in the class. Crowe trusted Saunders's credibility, so he tipped the Federal Bureau of Inves-

tigation (FBI). Other people later came forward with their own tales of Eckardt's involvement in the crime.

Harding implicates Gillooly

Gillooly also became a target of the investigation. On January 18 Harding was interviewed by the FBI. When asked whether Gillooly was involved in the Kerrigan assault, she said no. After a conversation with her attorney during a break in the interview, however, Harding changed her testimony. She stated that she intended to leave Gillooly for good, and she definitely felt he was involved in the attack. Gillooly was arrested the next day. He later pleaded guilty to one count of racketeering (being part of a dishonest business enterprise), for which he received a two-year prison sentence and a fine of $100,000. During seventeen and a half hours of testimony he claimed that Harding was part of the plan to remove Kerrigan from Olympic competition. Nevertheless, Gillooly was not able to offer enough solid evidence to indict Harding on charges of pre-assault conspiracy. (A conspiracy is a secret plan to commit an unlawful act.) Two other people were also arrested for their involvement in the assault. Shane Stant, the man who actually struck Kerrigan, surrendered to the police. The second participant, Derrick Smith, was arrested and charged with conspiracy to commit assault.

The downfall of Tonya Harding

Harding was never charged in the incident. People who knew her well doubted that she could have been part of the plot. They said she was far more likely to enjoy beating her opponents legitimately on the ice. Despite the lack of evidence against Harding, the United States Figure Skating Association ruled that the skater had to face a disciplinary hearing. As part of the hearing process, the United States Olympic Committee reviewed the case. The committee eventually ruled in Harding's favor and she was allowed to skate in the games. Harding, however, was still under a cloud of suspicion. The speculation surrounding the Kerrigan incident followed her to the

◀ Tonya Harding (right) and Nancy Kerrigan share some ice time. Harding later became a suspect in an attack on Kerrigan during a championship skating meet in Detroit, Michigan.

Olympics, where she gave a disappointing performance. Despite her earlier injury, Kerrigan was also able to compete and won a silver medal. No matter what her role may or may not have been in the Kerrigan attack, Harding had lost her long-desired medal, as well as the respect of the figure skating community and fans around the world.

FOR FURTHER REFERENCE

Periodicals

Brownlee, Shannon. "Surrealism on the Ice." *U.S. News & World Report.* January 24, 1994.

Smolowe, Jill. "The Slippery Saga of Tonya Harding." *Time.* February 14, 1994.

Nicholas Leeson and the Collapse of Barings PLC

1995

Because of Nicholas Leeson's financial scheming—and Barings's lack of attention to his activities—a centuries-old institution was devastated.

Nicholas Leeson was a promising young trader with Baring Future Singapore when he rocked the financial industry with a daring—and totally irresponsible—feat. In 1995 he triggered the collapse of Barings PLC, an old and prestigious British financial institution. As a result of his reckless trading procedures, Leeson caused the company to lose over $2 billion and go out of business. The fall of such a respected establishment was met with shock around the world, especially in Britain. (Barings was one of the bankers for Queen Elizabeth II, who reportedly could have lost close to one million dollars in the disaster.) It was also the bank that financed the Louisiana Purchase in 1803. (The Louisiana Purchase was the sale of the Louisiana territory by France to the United States.) According to initial reports, Leeson had masterminded the scheme on his own. But most observers suspected that some Barings officials knew about his activities from the start. The fall of Barings provided an example of how financial institutions must learn to adapt to a rapidly changing world.

Barings enters new market

Prior to the 1980s, banks offered such traditional services as checking accounts, savings accounts, loans, and financial advice. Then banking institutions began moving into stock trading, which had previously been a separate industry. By the late 1980s most large banks had established divisions that employed traders. (A trader is a person who buys and sells stocks and commodities futures. A stock is a share in a company. A commodities future is an item sold for future delivery.) In the 1990s an even newer form of trading, called derivatives, emerged in the financial world. (A derivative is a form of a bet on the stock market. The procedure is much like placing a bet on whether the final score of a football game will be above or below a certain number of points. In the case of a derivative, a trader advises a client to place a bet on, for example, how much a particular stock will be worth on a certain date.)

In addition to introducing yet another dimension to banking, derivatives required a different kind of employee—one who could operate computers, take daring risks, and keep track of fast-paced global stock exchanges. (A stock exchange is a place where stock trading is conducted on an organized system.) Among the banks that decided to become involved in derivatives trading was Barings PLC, a venerable institution based in London, England. One of the traders Barings appointed to its derivatives office was Nicholas Leeson, a young man from a working-class background who had skipped college to go directly into banking.

Leeson seizes opportunity

Leeson began his Barings career in 1989 as a clerk at the London office. He did settlement work (keeping account of income from the settling of legal cases), making sure all transactions were recorded and paid. At that time, Barings was in the process of determining whether to enter the derivatives market. Leeson took advantage of this opportunity to learn as much as he could about derivatives so he could be part of Barings's future. He advanced quickly in the corporation, and in 1992 was moved to the job of roving troubleshooter (a person who helps solve problems). Barings sent Leeson to Indonesia (a country in southeast Asia) and Tokyo, Japan, to set up offices. Ironically, he was also in charge of investigating internal fraud (the intentional misuse of funds by someone within the company).

At the same time, the Singapore International Monetary Exchange (SIMEX) was becoming Asia's foremost financial market. Barings saw an opportunity to make money in Singapore by trading in derivatives. Leeson was sent to Singapore as a member of the team that would set up Baring Future Singapore (BFS). Soon BFS was understaffed, and Leeson began conducting derivatives deals himself. At the age of only twenty-five, he now had the complete confidence of Barings officials. It was an ideal chance for him to take advantage of the bank's inexperience in the derivatives market and advance his own career.

Works without supervision

Within a short time, Leeson was making the company tens of millions of dollars. His immediate boss was so impressed with his performance that he was allowed to work unsupervised. Not everyone was so quick to praise the young trader. Other traders warned SIMEX authorities that Leeson should be watched closely. Leeson seemed to believe that he could not lose, however, and he enjoyed every moment of his phenomenal success. In 1994, a Barings banker based in New York City introduced Leeson to a client whose identity remained anonymous. (The client would simply be referred to as account No. 88888.)

Makes risky bets

The stage was set for catastrophe when Leeson began making open-ended (unlimited) bets on billions of dollars worth of Japanese stocks and bonds (interest-bearing certificates). In Singapore, traders initially have to pay only a small percentage of a wager. (A wager is the amount of money placed as a bet. Paying only a percentage of the wager is similar to making a down payment or deposit on a purchase.) Therefore, losses could be quite heavy if a trader made a losing bet and the bank had to pay the balance (the rest of the amount owed on the

On November 23, 1995, ex-Barings trader Nicholas Leeson (far left, in baseball cap) arrives in Singapore after his arrest on multiple charges of fraud and forgery.

wager). Barings officials believed the company was not at risk, however, because Leeson was supposedly using his clients' funds for the bets. He also seemed to be making a profit in cases when he did use the bank's money. For a few months no one was the wiser to Leeson's ways.

In late November 1994, Leeson bet that the Nikkei index would not drop below 19,000 points on March 10, 1995. (Nikkei is the Japanese stock exchange. An index is the total number of points that all stocks rise or fall.) The Japanese economy was improving and the bet seemed to be a safe one. Then on January 11, 1995, when Leeson's bet was still secure, an earthquake struck the Japanese city of Kobe. The Nikkei index plummeted. Amazingly, Lesson continued to assume a "can't lose" attitude and placed even more wagers. He decided that the Nikkei would eventually stabilize, but made no other plans to protect losses that Barings and mystery client No. 88888 might suffer if the index remained low. This was a fatal mistake.

Barings warned

As early as 1992 Barings officials had warned that BFS could be losing money or client confidence, and possibly both, on derivatives trading. For some reason, though, Leeson was still trading with no supervision from his superiors. The Barings employee-monitoring system seemed to support his activities. Then a BFS internal audit (a review of client accounts and transactions) in 1994 revealed Leeson to be a risk. Yet Barings officials assumed Leeson's losses were related to the unpredictable nature of the derivatives market and not to any irresponsibility on his part. Managers still saw no reason for serious concern. From October 1993 until January 1, 1995, Leeson remained free to continue his reckless activities.

In January 1995 Barings headquarters sent a troubleshooter to Singapore to tell Leeson and his team to be more cautious in making derivatives wagers. On February 20, Leeson was asked by his regional supervisors in Tokyo to reduce the company's holdings of Nikkei contracts (agreements that state the terms of the wagers). But it was too late: The extended credit (money loaned by Barings to a customer) for account No. 88888 had exceeded the bank's capital (the amount of money Barings had available) by $2 billion. Shortly thereafter, Barings PLC collapsed.

Leeson disappears

Many of Leeson's colleagues later recalled that in the weeks before his downfall he did not seem to be himself. He was throwing up in the bathroom, and appeared to be extremely distracted. Yet he was still boasting about the huge bonus he was expecting. No one detected any warning signs of what was to come, primarily because Leeson was a very private person. For instance, few of his fellow traders knew he was married. In retrospect, it was obvious that the Leesons knew the end was near, and they had made preparations. Lisa Leeson had called a moving company to put their belongings into storage. Leeson had sold his black Rover sports car, and he was leasing a white Mercedes. By Friday, February 24, the Leesons had disappeared. Soon after Leeson left Singapore, he faxed a letter to the chairman of the bank, Peter Baring. In the letter he apologized for his actions and gave details about what he had done.

Leeson goes to prison

Meanwhile, the Leesons had flown to Malaysia (a country in southeast Asia), then to Brunei, Borneo. On March 1, they boarded a flight for Frankfurt, Germany, en route to London. German authorities boarded the plane in Frankfurt and took the couple into custody. Lisa Leeson was later released. (It has been speculated, however, that she may have been involved in Nicholas's scheme. She had worked in a BFS back (clerical) office, where all trading transactions were processed and monitored. Therefore she could have helped her husband hide his gambling from Barings senior managers.) After Leeson was detained in Germany he immediately stated that he did not steal any money. Furthermore, he claimed that his bosses were fully aware of the scheme.

Leeson made an appeal to British prime minister John Major to be extradited (returned to stand trial) to England. Leeson wanted to avoid being tried in Singapore, where laws are extremely strict. However, Britain's Serious Fraud Office denied his appeal and the German court ordered him to return to Singapore. On October 17, Singapore authorities released a report that accused Barings senior management of trying to conceal Leeson's trading activities. When Leeson arrived in Singapore, he was arrested as soon as he stepped off the plane. On December 1, Leeson pleaded guilty to two charges of fraud. He was sentenced to six and one-half years in jail.

Barings unprepared for new world

The Barings collapse affected many employees who were about to receive bonuses. To make matters worse, it was tax time and their salaries were being held. Although Barings officials frantically searched for a rescuer, they failed to find any other institution that would agree to take on the huge debt resulting from the collapse. Thus 232-year-old Barings PLC was completely brought down.

The trading world was left shocked in the wake of this financial calamity. Experts could not understand why a respected institution like Barings would permit an inexperienced trader to assume so much responsibility. Derivatives was an untested trading market, they argued, and even seasoned professionals were often unable to comprehend its complexity. Despite the promise Leeson had shown in other areas of banking, at the age of twenty-eight he did not have enough experience to know when to cut his losses. Even more unbelievably, Barings managers had given him free rein for almost a year and a half, leaving him unsupervised until it was too late. As a result, Leeson's scheming—and Barings's inability to monitor his activities—devastated a centuries-old institution. In the aftermath of the Barings collapse, British banking regulators took steps to ensure better training of traders and closer supervision of trading procedures.

Working-class hero?

During Leeson's trial, the media portrayed him as a "working-class hero" because he grew up in public housing and did not go to college. Social critics said he was out of place at Barings PLC, which catered to upper-class clients and usually hired only graduates of elite universities. Industry analysts charged that Barings managers had made Leeson a convenient scapegoat, calling him a rogue (isolated and uncontrollable) trader so they would not have to take the blame for the collapse of the company.

Many observers noted that Leeson was a typical employee on the financial frontier. The problem, they noted, was actually a generation gap. The world was changing at a dizzying pace, causing traditional banking procedures, along with bankers wearing pinstripe suits and bowler hats, to become outmoded. Suits had been replaced by T-shirts and jeans, and the baseball cap was now the preferred headgear. Firms were recruiting derivatives traders, and they were generally energetic, self-confident young people who created a casual and chaotic work environment. These traders had grown up using a computer (the tool of the derivatives market), thrived on living on the edge, and enjoyed taking risks. Unlike their older, more conservative colleagues, they were not especially concerned about proper social behavior and they often valued experience over education. Thus the story of Nicholas Leeson became a lesson for traditionalists who failed to adjust to a new era.

FOR FURTHER REFERENCE

Periodicals

Powell, Bill, Daniel Pederson, and Michael Elliott. "Busted!" *Newsweek.* March 13, 1995, pp. 36–42.

Wallace, Bruce. "Cultural Differences." *Maclean's.* March 20, 1995, pp. 32–33.

The Tokyo Nerve Gas Strike

MARCH 20, 1995

The Tokyo subway attack raised fears about the possible use of germ warfare in public areas.

O
n March 20, 1995, just after the 8:00 A.M. rush hour, vinyl bags containing nerve gas were placed on trains on three subway lines in Tokyo, Japan. Within minutes the gas completely engulfed the trains, killing at least twelve people. Thousands more were injured. Sixteen subway stations were targeted in the attack, including those serving the National Parliament and the Foreign Ministry. No group accepted immediate responsibility, but authorities concluded that the action was a terrorist strike. Although there had been previous random acts of terrorism in Japan, the incident in the subway did not fit past patterns. Days later, government investigators identified the attackers, an obscure sect called "Aum Shinrikyo" that was headed by Shoko Asahara. After Asahara was arrested he announced that the government's efforts to demolish his movement coincided with the beginning of the end of the world. The Tokyo subway attack raised fears about germ warfare use on the general public.

Shoko Asahara

Shoko Asahara (1955–) was born Chizuo Matsumoto on Kyushu (one of Japan's main islands, south of Honshu). From birth Asahara was blind in one eye and partially blind in the other. When he was six years old his father sent him to a school

711

for the blind. Asahara had an advantage over his classmates in that he had partial sight. Remembered as a bully, Asahara often chastised other students and conned them into buying him dinner in exchange for his taking them out. He was also guilty of other delinquent acts, such as threatening to burn down the dormitory and breaking the eardrum of another student. In 1978 Asahara married Tomoko Ishii and opened an apothecary (pharmacy) specializing in traditional Chinese medicines. Four years later, Asahara was arrested for selling fake cures and his business went bankrupt.

Asahara established Aum Shinrikyo in 1987. A mixture of many disciplines, the religion is based on combating a supposed United States conspiracy that uses sex and junk food as weapons. As his religion expanded around the world, Asahara accumulated great wealth. He became more paranoid than ever and consumed with a sense of danger. Asahara predicted the end of the world between 1997 and 2000, and kept his devotees in check by making them bow and kiss his toe. During the 1990s the cult attracted many wealthy and educated members. Soon Aum was operating discount stores, coffee shops, and a personal-computer assembly factory. By 1994 Aum had thirty Japanese branches with 10,000 members and many international offices. (The Russian branch alone boasted between 10,000 and 40,000 members.)

Many families were vocal about losing their loved ones to the cult. Cult practices include self-starvation, immersion in very hot or very cold water, and drug ingestion. Cult members were also expected to hand over their financial assets. As a former Aum follower commented, "They [the cult leaders] promise you heaven, but they make you live in hell."

Sarin released into subway

On the morning of March 20, 1995, a man wearing large sunglasses, brown trousers, a beige or blue coat, and a surgical mask boarded a train on the Tokyo subway line. Passengers watched as the man fiddled with a foot-long rectangular object wrapped in newspapers. He left the package in a plastic bag on the floor when he got off at the next stop. Unsuspecting passengers soon noticed oily water on the floor near the bag, and they detected an awful odor. Within moments, a chilling episode began to unfold as gas, later identified as sarin, seeped into the train. People scrambled out of the cars with their eyes and mouths covered. Many passengers had lost their voices and could not scream, while others were in a numbed state.

As it turned out, the bag was one of several left on three subway lines, and this terrifying scene was taking place on fifteen other trains. The Tokyo Fire Department responded with 340 units and 1,364 personnel. By the time rescue squads reached the disaster sites, thousands of people had been overcome by the fumes. Most were vomiting and collapsing. Rescue workers themselves suffered the effects of the gas. The number of casualties was calculated at 5,510; at least twelve people died. Hundreds of people were temporarily blinded. The incident horrified Japanese citizens, who pride themselves on their crime-free environment. In the aftermath of the attack, many people expressed their fear of riding the subway.

Aum Shinrikyo suspected

Sarin gas was developed by the Nazi government in Germany during World War II (1939–45) as part of its germ warfare arsenal. The gas was made by combining chemicals such a fluorine and organic phosphorous. It attacked the central nervous system. Since sarin is not available legally in Japan, the government immediately reacted to the incident by increasing security at all railways, airports, and seaports. At first authorities were unable to implicate anyone in the attack. Within days, however, Japan's national police deployed 2,500 troops to the offices of Aum Shinrikyo. The police said that the official reason was investigation of a kidnapping, but preparations for this investigation suggested they expected something more.

Chemicals found

At twenty-five Aum Shinrikyo branches around the country, canaries were released into offices while over 1,000 policemen waited outside in protective suits with gas monitoring equipment. (Canaries are small birds that have traditionally been used by miners to test the purity of the air in mines. Canaries will show signs of distress in the presence of a deadly gas more quickly than humans.) The birds lived, thus indicating it was safe for the police to enter the buildings. Members of the cult, however, seemed to expect the arrival of the police.

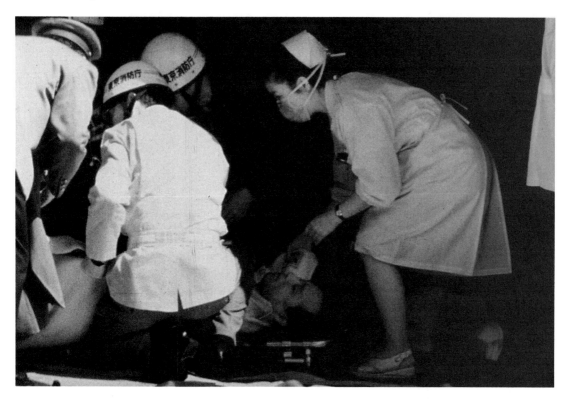

Paramedic teams treat injured passengers after a deadly sarin gas strike on the Tokyo subway. Twelve people were killed and over five thousand passengers were injured in the attack.

They agreed to cooperate even though they felt the search was unjust. Many members were found under blankets in small cubicles suffering from malnutrition, although others claimed that they were fasting voluntarily.

For days, the police carried out tons of chemicals. Some were benign (not harmful), others could be toxic (poisonous) if mixed, and many were deadly on their own. Aum members explained that the chemicals were used for making pottery and processing semiconductors (electronic devices in computer systems) for their business. While these purposes were possibly legitimate, the amount of the chemicals was suspect. The police decided it was time to question Aum guru Asahara himself.

Asahara proclaims innocence

Asahara proclaimed his innocence, and his lawyers echoed his statements. He released two radio messages, saying in a singsong voice, "I didn't do it. I'm innocent," over and over again. He also directed his disciples to "face death without regrets." His lawyer responded with a more practical approach, saying that the Aum Shinrikyo religion was based on nonviolence, so the cult could not possibly be involved. Asahara instead pointed a finger at the United States military, which had the ability to make sarin. Despite these efforts Asahara and several other cult members were arrested. To justify the arrests, police revealed that they were investigating over 110 complaints against the cult for such offenses as unlawful confinement, assault, and theft.

The charges were legitimate and stemmed from past incidents in which involvement of the cult was suspected. In 1989, for instance, an attorney took the case of a family searching for a son who had joined Aum. Five months later, the entire family disappeared. When another man tried to prevent his wealthy sister from giving Aum the building in which his office was located, four men later grabbed him. He had not been seen since. Still another incident involving the cult was a land dispute in the city of Matsumoto. Three weeks before the decision was to be made, a cloud of sarin was released in the city at night. Seven people were killed and many were hospitalized. The three judges deciding the case were sleeping in the affected area, and a decision was never issued.

Fears of another attack

Almost a week after the incident, most of the survivors of the gassing were able to leave the hospital. At the same time, many other people were coming to hospitals claiming they had been gassed. Asahara, meanwhile, had kept a low profile. He released a videotape in which he supposedly answered questions, but he simply reiterated his previous explanations. The guru also released a videotape to his cult members, claiming that they were the object of a poison-gas attack, whose origin was "unmistakably" the United States. During the effort to link Aum Shinrikyo to the subway incident, many Japanese officials feared a revenge attack. Asahara and his cult disciples were later charged and tried; the trial was continuing in 1998. Nevertheless, the Tokyo tragedy had taken a severe toll on Japanese citizens, who were accustomed to living in a society based on mutual trust and good will.

New facts revealed

In May 1998 *The New York Times* published new revelations about Aum Shinrikyo and the sarin strike on the Tokyo subway. *Times* reporters reviewed transcripts of the trial of Aum cult members and interviewed Japanese investigators who were still working on the case. Newly released evidence showed that during the early 1990s, the cult had made at least eight other attacks with germs of the diseases anthrax and botulism. Aum apparently wanted to take over the world, and his group's main strategy was to start a terrible war with the release of biological substances into the environment.

In addition to releasing sarin into the Tokyo subway in 1995, Aum had sprayed toxic chemicals from rooftops and from trucks. Among the targeted locations were the Japanese Diet (legislature), the emperor's palace, the city of Tokyo, and the U.S. naval base at Yokosuka. No one was killed, and Japanese authorities were investigating whether there had been any effects from the attacks. In fact, the only victims may have been Aum members themselves. Members manufactured chemicals under the direction of Seiichi Endo, a former graduate student in biology, who was given the Aum title of "biological weapons chief." Endo's job was to locate and reproduce lethal germs, then turn them into a form that could be easily dispersed. Aum preferred a mist or powder that would quickly penetrate human lungs, but Endo had to resort to using a gas in the subway attack. The only reason the Tokoyo tragedy and the other strikes were not more deadly was that the cult had not yet gotten hold of a strong enough germ.

FOR FURTHER REFERENCE

Periodicals

Broad, William, and Sheryl WuDunn and Judith Miller. "How Japan Germ Terror Alerted World." *The New York Times.* May 26, 1998, pp. A1, A10.

Hostage Crisis in Peru

DECEMBER 17, 1996 TO APRIL 13, 1997

O n the evening of December 17, 1996, the Tupac Amaru Revolutionary Movement (MRTA) staged a surprise attack on the Japanese embassy in Lima, Peru. The Tupac Amaru and their leader, Nestor Cerpa Cartolini, quickly established control of the embassy. The rebels' goal was to use the hostages to gain release of over 400 MRTA members held in Peruvian prisons. During negotiations with government officials, the Tupac Amaru released a series of communiqués (official statements) explaining its position. The talks were complicated for the Peruvian government because the embassy was on Japanese sovereign land, so any negotiations required the involvement of the Japanese government. Peruvian president Alberto Fujimori (1938–), who is of Japanese descent, had depended upon Japanese economic support to strengthen his regime in Peru. Nevertheless, Fujimori took a hard-line position in dealing with the MRTA, whom he considered terrorists. Fujimori's actions went against the moderate approach favored by the Japanese. The hostage crisis lasted for 126 days, and the MRTA was able to command the world's attention to its cause. From the beginning, however, the raid was doomed to failure. It ended badly for the MRTA insurgents and triumphantly for Fujimori.

Revolutionary Nestor Cerpa thought he could simply take hostages, make demands, and force Fujimori to accept his terms.

Embassy party disrupted

The Tupac Amaru surprise attack on the Japanese ambassador's residence on December 17, 1996, resulted in the capture of 500 dignitaries who were attending a celebration of the emperor's birthday. Among the guests were diplomats, government officials, and relatives of Fujimori, including his mother, sister, and brother. At 8:30 P.M., a loud explosion blew a hole in the wall of the embassy compound. A group of fourteen guerrilla fighters stormed into the building and soon gained control of a hostage population that outnumbered them twenty-five to one. Cerpa, the rebel leader, expected half of his small fighting force to be killed in the assault, but only one of them was hurt. Considering the status of his captives and their roles in enforcing government policy, the move had been especially daring. The attack immediately created an international platform for Cerpa's demands.

Tupac Amaru issues demands

The next day Cerpa released all of the women and many of the elderly men. American hostages were also released to avoid any involvement on the part of the United States government. Over the next few days other hostages were freed until a core group of seventy-two people remained. In its first communiqué the Tupac Amaru announced that it had given the operation the name "Oscar Torres Condesu," with the slogan "Breaking the Silence—the Peoples Want Them Free." The guerrilla unit in the embassy compound was called "Edgar Sanchez." The Tupac Amaru demanded the release of MRTA members—especially women—held in Peruvian prisons, which the rebels described as "grave prisons." The group also condemned Japanese influence in Peru.

During the hostage crisis the rebels issued a constant flurry of statements, repeating their demands. They lashed out at journalists who had criticized the MRTA, and they denounced the Peruvian government as undemocratic. Although the Tupac rebels received international attention, they gained hardly any sympathy for their actions. Governments throughout the world expressed support for Fujimori. Amnesty International (an organization that specializes in furthering human rights worldwide) and the Inter-American Commission on Human Rights (CIDH) condemned the MRTA for taking hostages and violating their rights.

Digging of tunnels

The government of Peru immediately tried to reach a political solution with the MRTA. Japanese and Peruvian officials traveled to the Dominican Republic and to Cuba to arrange possible asylum (relocation to a sympathetic country) for the rebels. Cerpa never wavered in his demand for the release of 400 prisoners. Likewise, Fujimori refused to compromise, although he did tell Cerpa that he wanted a peaceful end to the crisis. A potential agreement fell through in March, however, when Cerpa called a halt to the negotiations. He suspected that Fujimori had authorized the digging of tunnels under the embassy, and he saw this action as a prelude to an assault. This development wounded the talks, which never recovered in any meaningful way.

Cerpa was right: The government had indeed dug a tunnel system and was planning to launch a surprise attack. Fujimori had tried to disguise the sounds of digging by broadcasting loud music. Professional miners had been brought to Lima to do the digging. The miners worked in four-man teams on four-hour shifts under the code name "Chavin de Huantar" (a reference to a pre-Inca archaeological site with underground passageways). Two main tunnels branched out with three others to reach strategic spots under the embassy mansion. Any rescue

Peruvian and Japanese police investigators meet outside the Japanese ambassador's residence to collect evidence after the end of the MRTA hostage crisis.

plan would draw the scrutiny of the Japanese government, however, which had become suspicious of police actions outside the embassy. The officials were fearful of Japanese hostages being harmed and did not want any extreme measures taken to free the captives. As early as February, Peruvian and Japanese officials had met in Canada. Japanese diplomats wanted a guarantee that the Peruvians would not attempt an attack on the embassy without prior approval from Japan.

Government plans assault

The Peruvian government and security forces had carefully planned the assault. They used a variety of methods for identifying the location of the captors and guiding the strike. A listening device, hidden in a guitar, had been smuggled into the embassy. Other listening devices—some as small as match heads with twenty-day batteries—were also concealed in goods sent to hostages from relatives. A retired navy admiral had kept a radio receiver hidden from the guerrillas. Through the Red Cross relatives sent light-colored clothes for the hostages to wear. This would make the captives' clothing stand out from the olive-green uniforms of the guerrillas, so that they could easily be identified by their rescuers when the strike took place.

Commandos invade embassy

One hundred forty commandos (specially trained assault soldiers) were preparing to rescue the hostages. The commandos had rehearsed their operation in two full-scale mockups (replicas) of the embassy. They wore Israeli helmets and body armor, which had been supplied to Peru by Israeli antiterrorism experts in the 1980s. On April 13, 1997, the day of the attack, the commandos knew exactly where to go once they moved through the tunnels and emerged into the embassy.

Peruvian intelligence had determined that about six guerrillas had begun playing soccer in the first-floor banquet hall. At 3:17 P.M., nine pounds of plastic explosives were detonated from the tunnel under the banquet hall floor, instantly killing some of the rebel soccer players. A second charge was detonated in the tunnel beneath the room used by the guerrillas for their headquarters. From the other three tunnels, commandos popped up through the floors. At the same time, a military

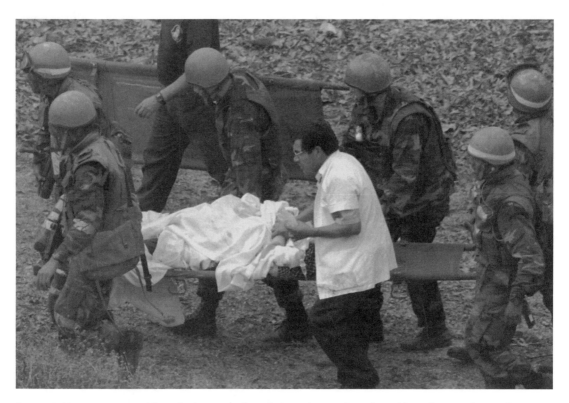

A wounded hostage is removed from the Japanese ambassador's residence in Lima, Peru. After a four-month seige, Peruvian commandos stormed the compound and killed most of the guerrillas.

police team broke through the embassy front gate and blew open the front door. Other commandos attacked from the rear, while still others climbed onto the roof.

All rebels killed

Ten minutes earlier, hostages with military connections had received a message (the playing of a march at a nearby army base) that the rescue was imminent. The military men then warned the other captives, telling them to stay on the floor and not to move. At the time of the assault Cerpa and four or five guerrillas were possibly asleep or watching the soccer game. When the commandos burst through the floor of the banquet hall, Cerpa and his comrades tried to get to the second floor where the hostages were being guarded by two or three other guerrillas. Cerpa fired his gun once, and then he was fatally shot. All fourteen guerrillas were killed by the commandos, and the 126-day hostage crisis ended. (Critics later charged that many rebels had been executed, in clear violation of the law.) Two Peruvian soldiers died from bullet wounds.

The only hostage to die was Carlos Giusi, a supreme court judge, who sustained a leg wound. Complications from the wound caused Giusi to have a heart attack. One of the captives told an American journalist that a rebel held a gun to his head but did not pull the trigger. Many hostages praised Fujimori's decision and expressed no sympathy for the guerrillas. Unlike other hostage-takers, the Tupac Amaru had made no attempt to gain the trust of their captives.

Fujimori triumphs

Fujimori was a hero after the invasion. He had orchestrated an assault that, in years to come, would be studied as an effective tactic for combating terrorism. Fujimori had won many victories in his career: He had defeated Peruvian novelist Mario Vargas Llosa (1936–) in the 1990 presidential election, he had initiated successful market reforms, and he had won reelection in 1995. Yet the hostage rescue was perhaps his finest hour.

Fujimori later toured the Japanese embassy, the site of his triumph. Outside the walls, he climbed onto the hood of an automobile and shouted, "We will never give in to terrorist blackmail!" Having always taken a hard line against rebels, Fujimori did not consult Japanese diplomats before ordering the assault. His results, however, could not be faulted by the Japanese government, since not a single Japanese hostage was killed. Cerpa had also underestimated Fujimori's resolve. He apparently thought that he could take hostages, make demands, and force the president to accept his terms. He had made no plans, however, for defending his guerrillas against a possible attack. In the end, Cerpa's little band was no match for highly trained commandos who had no intention of taking prisoners.

FOR FURTHER REFERENCE

Periodicals

"Japanese Embassy Siege Ended in Surprise Strike." International Press Service. April 22, 1997.

Lama, Abraham. "Peru: Fujimori Versus MRTA Drags on as Tension Grows." International Press Service. December 20, 1996.

The Bre-X Scandal

1997

The Bre-X gold strike scandal stands as a classic misadventure that resulted from deception, negligence, and greed.

In 1993 a group of Canadian prospectors issued a public report stating that they had struck gold in a remote part of Indonesia (a country in southeast Asia). The report said that millions of years ago a volcano had collapsed, and the resulting heat and pressure had created a large deposit of gold. The prospectors also claimed that it was the largest deposit of gold in the history of the world, worth over $70 billion. This announcement caused such widespread hysteria among investors that the event was even greater than the California Gold Rush of 1848. (The California Gold Rush resulted from the discovery of gold on January 24, 1848, at Sutter's Mill in Coloma, California. Although 40,000 prospectors converged on the site within a period of two years, few of them struck it rich. The gold strike, however, triggered economic growth in the area.)

Later that year two of the prospectors created the Bre-X Mining company in Canada. Money came pouring in from investors. Then reality set in. Four years later, after the Bre-X founders had gotten rich, the entire venture was revealed as a scam—there was no gold. Investors who had swarmed to the project lost all their money, and the Indonesians who were hired to dig up the gold lost their jobs. The Bre-X scandal stands as a classic misadventure that resulted from deception, negligence, and greed.

Geologists "strike gold"

The story behind the Bre-X scandal is full of mystery. The scandal began in 1988 on the island of Borneo (a remote island belonging to Indonesia) where some Australian geologists witnessed Dayaks (Christian tribespeople of Borneo) panning for gold. After the Australians decided there might be gold on the island, they began speculative mining. A year later, the geologists drilled nineteen core samples (cylinders containing soil and minerals) and discovered a small amount of gold. Unfortunately, it was not enough gold to convince any mining company to come to Borneo and dig for more. In order for the geologists to fund an expensive mining project, they would need the support of a large corporation.

Bre-X created

Since the Australian geologists could not turn their prospects into riches, they decided not to proceed. In fact, everyone gave up except for two men on the team, Philippine geologist Michael De Guzman and Dutch-born Canadian businessman John Felderhof. The two men suddenly came forward and announced that they had struck gold in Busang (a village in Borneo). In fact, De Guzman and Felderhof claimed not only to have struck gold, but to have found the largest deposit of gold in the history of the world.

Canadian stockbroker David Walsh was the president of Bre-X Mining. Up until his death in 1998, Walsh continued to claim that he did not know about a plan to swindle investors in the company's Borneo gold operation.

Because gold is naturally buried deep in the ground, it was difficult to know whether or not De Guzman and Felderhof were lying. The only way to find out was to dig up the gold. Unlike the Australians, De Guzman and Felderhof had no trouble finding support for this effort. Felderhof had connections with former Canadian stockbroker David Walsh, who could not wait to strike it rich. Eventually Walsh's wife raised $250,000 to start a mining company that was large enough to take on an immense mining project. Walsh was named president of the new company. Thus, in 1993 Bre-X was born, and mining in Busang began.

DE GUZMAN: MASTERMIND OR PAWN?

After the Bre-X hoax was revealed on May 12, 1997, officials were amazed at how well the scam had been orchestrated. The chief executive officer of Freeport McMoRan Copper and Gold, James R. Moffett, was instrumental in ending the swindle. An experienced leader of the New Orleans mining firm, Moffett explained that all core samples must represent a real deposit of gold in order to be considered legitimate. Noting how convincing the fake Bre-X samples were, he said they had to be produced by a very skillful geologist. The only member of the Bre-X team with this kind of knowledge was Michael De Guzman.

By the time the scam was revealed, however, De Guzman was dead. At 10:30 A.M. on March 19, 1997, he was enroute to Busang, Borneo, the site of the supposed gold discovery, in the Bre-X helicopter. During the flight, De Guzman apparently jumped or was pushed from the helicopter and plummeted 800 feet into the dense jungle below. Four days later a body was found in the jungle, but it had been so devoured by wild animals that it was very hard to identify. A coroner finally matched a mangled thumbprint with an identification card that belonged to De Guzman.

The timing of De Guzman's death suggests that he was the man who orchestrated the Bre-X scandal. Investigators have speculated that he may have been murdered so he would not reveal the truth, or he may have committed suicide so he would not be held responsible for the scam. There is no conclusive evidence, however, to support either claim. De Guzman's associates vouch for the fact that he was a smart man who was perfectly capable of pulling off a stunt such as the fake gold strike. (De Guzman himself claimed to have an IQ of 150 to 170.) Nevertheless, the Bre-X scam remains a mystery, and De Guzman's death leaves behind many unanswered questions.

Bre-X salts samples

For the sake of appearance, the mining camp that the Bre-X partners installed at Busang looked authentic. They set up modern buildings equipped with satellite phones and faxes so that the geologists could remain in contact with the outside world. The company also had its own helicopter, complete with a helipad for landings. In addition to employing 400 Dayaks to dig up the gold, Bre-X spent more than $1 million on a social development program that included a school to educate children in the area. As a result, from an outsider's perspective, Busang appeared to be a thriving operation. On the inside, however, work of a very different sort was apparently going on.

When the Bre-X scandal was later revealed in 1997, it was found that workers were digging up something, but not the largest gold deposit in the world. In order to prove there was gold at the Busang site, De Guzman and Felderhof sent core samples to a local laboratory in Samarinda, Indonesia, to be inspected by an assayer (a person who appraises core samples) in 1993. The samples contained gold, but not from the Busang site. This fact was not discovered until it was too late. In the meantime, De Guzman and Felderhof continued to fool assayers by allegedly "salting" (manually depositing gold from an outside source) the samples.

Bre-X lures investors

In order to lure investors, Felderhof made public announcements about the amount of potential wealth at the Busang site. In 1993, after Bre-X first opened its doors, Felderhof claimed that there were about 30 million ounces of gold buried at the site. Over time, Felderhof apparently embellished the truth so much that by the end of the scam in 1997, the amount of gold had supposedly grown to 200 million ounces. According to Felderhof's account, the largest deposit of gold in the history of the world was worth $70 billion.

Not surprisingly, between 1993 and 1997 investors from all over the world poured money into Bre-X. As a result, Bre-X stock soared from being worth pennies in 1993, to $200 a share in September of 1996. If $70 billion worth of gold were ever dug up, these investors would have become very rich. Instead, because of all the investments in Bre-X, the only people getting rich from Busang were De Guzman, Felderhof, and Walsh.

Respected companies support venture

There were many victims of the Bre-X scandal who expected to make a lot of money but ended up with nothing. While many private citizens spent their life savings on Bre-X stock, most of the investors were large companies from the United States, Canada, and Indonesia. For example, the biggest investor in the Bre-X scam was Fidelity Investments of Boston, Massachusetts. Fidelity managed to make some money and then bail out before Bre-X went under. A well-known investment bank, J.P. Morgan, even acted as a Bre-X adviser. The most significant investor, however, was Freeport

McMoRan Copper and Gold, a mining company based in New
Orleans, Louisiana. Freeport McMoRan joined the Bre-X operation as a partner in February of 1997, and promised to spend
a total of $1.2 billion on the project. Ironically, it was Freeport
McMoRan that ended up being instrumental in exposing the
entire scam.

Bre-X exposed

In March 1997, one month after joining the operation,
Freeport McMoRan officials became suspicious about the honesty of Bre-X. As rumors about a possible scam spread to other
investors, a scandal began to develop and panic broke out.
The result was that the value of Bre-X stock dropped from
$200 a share to $2 a share. Bre-X responded by having core
samples checked once again, but this time the sample tests
failed. The company then hired Strathcona Mineral Services of
Toronto, Canada, who concluded that the samples had been
salted. Freeport McMoRan also did some digging at the site.
As could be expected, their samples contained absolutely no
gold. Finally, on May 12, 1997, the verdict was in: Bre-X was
a scam, and the largest deposit of gold in the history of the
world did not exist.

Bre-X partners profit

Apparently, Bre-X got away with salting the samples the first time because the inspection was done locally. Borneo is a remote area, and nobody wanted to take the initiative to verify the core samples by coming to the island. When Bre-X tried to get away with salting the second time, however, the plan failed because the company was dealing with a larger institution with more sophisticated equipment. Interestingly, the Bre-X partners still enjoyed some nice profits. For instance, Walsh and his wife made $20 million from the scam, and Felderhof made $29 million. De Guzman, on the other hand, was less fortunate. After fake samples had been identified by Strathcona, De Guzman allegedly jumped (or was pushed) from the Bre-X helicopter on March 19, 1997, possibly taking all of the scam's secrets with him. American investors were protected by institutions such as the Securities and Exchange Commission, which investigates scams. But investors in the rest of the world had little defense against the deception and still lost their money.

FOR FURTHER REFERENCE

Periodicals

Behar, Richard. "Jungle Fever." *Fortune.* June 9, 1997, pp. 120–24, 128.

Wells, Jennifer. "Body of Evidence." *Maclean's,* August 8, 1997, pp. 40–43.

Other

"Bre-X Scandal Haunts Former President Even at Death." [CNN Online] Available http://cnn.com/WORLD/americas, June 5, 1998.

Picture Credits

The photographs and illustrations appearing in *Great Misadventures: Bad Ideas That Led to Big Disasters* were received from the following sources:

On the cover: *Titanic* sinking (**Painting by Willie Stoewer/UPI/Corbis-Bettmann. Reproduced by permission.**).

In the text: **Corbis-Bettmann. Reproduced by permission:** 4, 19, 35, 202, 218, 241, 284, 378, 389, 410, 447, 455, 468, 544, 586, 603; **Gustave Dore/Corbis-Bettmann. Reproduced by permission:** 10; **Archive Photos. Reproduced by permission:** 16, 27, 66, 97, 150, 153, 411, 412, 418, 436, 622, 652, 725; **Library of Congress. Reproduced by permission:** 42, 48, 105, 109, 231, 372, 406, 448, 464, 494, 565, 570, 578, 581, 588, 592, 628, 651; **The Granger Collection, New York. Reproduced by permission:** 56, 76, 115, 120, 123, 158; **Charles Nahl/Corbis-Bettmann. Reproduced by permission:** 91; **AP/Wide World Photos. Reproduced by permission:** 137, 142, 166, 176, 181, 186, 193, 210, 215, 245, 249, 257, 266, 267, 275, 290, 303, 305, 335, 339, 359, 361, 363, 367, 369, 452, 503, 505, 506, 514, 518, 530, 557, 602, 605, 630, 634, 642, 644, 646, 653, 662, 673, 682, 687, 697, 700, 706, 720, 722; **Norwegian Information Services. Reproduced by permission:** 154; **Lacy Atkins. AP/Wide World Photos. Reproduced by permission:** 176; **Archive Photos/Popperfoto. Reproduced by permission:** 200; **UPI/Corbis-Bettmann. Reproduced by permission:** 205, 226, 326, 544, 547, 616, 654; **Archive Photos/Lambert. Reproduced by permission:** 211; **Lisa Bunin/Greenpeace. Reproduced by permission:** 238; **Robert Visser/Greenpeace. Reproduced by permission:** 296; **Richard Diaz. AP/Wide World Photos. Reproduced by permission:** 303; **Peter Maksymec/AP/Wide World Photos.**

Index

C

C-16 Organized Crime Squad *4:* 684–85, 687, 688

CAA (Civil Aeronautics Administration) *2:* 259

CAB (Civil Aeronautics Board) *2:* 262–263

Cabeza de Vaca, Alvar Nuñez *1:* 34

Caesar and Cleopatra 4: 564

Caesarion *4:* 563

California Gold Rush *4:* 724

Californian 2: 206

Calley, William L. *3:* 541

Callisthenes *3:* 380

Calpurnia *4:* 563

Cameron, James *4:* 667

Cameron, Verney Lovett *1:* 113

Cantrill, Hadley *4:* 625

Carney, William H. *3:* 451

Carpathia 2: 206

Carrel, Alexis *2:* 214

Carson, Rachel *2:* 230, 232–34

Carter, Jimmy *2:* 238, 240, 242, 300; *3:* 546, 554

Cartolini, Nestor Cerpa *4:* 717–19, 722, 723

Casement, Roger *3:* 488, 491, 492, 492 (ill.), 494

Cass, Lewis *3:* 420–22

Castellano, Paul *4:* 689

Castro, Fidel *3:* 529, 530 (ill.), 531, 533

Catesby, Robert *4:* 580–82

Cayacauga 3: 417–19

Ceannt, Eamonn *3:* 489

Cecil, Edward *3:* 393, 395, 398

Center for the Biology of Natural Systems *2:* 280

Central Powers *3:* 470

CERN (European Laboratory for Particle Research) *2:* 314

Challenger explosion *2:* **320–30,** 321 (ill.), 326 (ill.)

Chambers, Whittaker *4:* 628

Chapin, Dwight *4:* 656

Charles I *4:* 580

Charles of Spain *1:*29, 31

Charles XII *3:* 400–02

Chase, Hal *4:* 609

Chaves, Steve *4:* 672

Chemical dispersants *2:* 340

Chemie Grünenthal *2:* 254–55

Chernobyl accident *2:* **331–37,** 335 (ill.)

Chevrolet Corvair *2:* **265–72,** 266 (ill.)

Chiang Kai-shek *4:* 629

Chicago White Sox *4:* 607, 610, 614

Chicksika *3:* 410

Child Pilot Safety Act *1:* 179

Children's Crusade *1:* **7–13,** 10 (ill.)

Christmas Island *1:* 73

Chrysler Valiant *2:* 267

Chuma, James *1:*110, 113

Churchill, Winston *3:* 500

Chuvakhin, Sergei *4:* 677, 678, 681

CIA (Central Intelligence Agency) *3:* 529, 532–34, 553, 558; *4:* 675, 680–83

Cicotte, Eddie *4:* 608, 610

Cimino, Michael *4:* 661, 662

Cincinnati Reds *4:* 607–09, 613, 614

Cirelli, Michael *4:* 686

Citizen Army *3:* 489

Citizen Kane 4: 624

Clark, William *1:* 89

Clark, Barney *2:* 214, 218 (ill.)

Clarke, Thomas *3:* 489–91

Clean Sox *4:* 607, 614

Cleopatra's fall *4:* **561–66,** 562 (ill.)

The Climb: Tragic Ambitions on Everest 1: 189

Clinton, Bill *1:* 175; *2:* 312, 349; *4:* 670

Clitus *3:* 380

CNN (Cable News Network) *3:* 558

Cobb, Ty *4:* 609, 613

Coiro, Michael *4:* 687

Colbern, Lawrence *3:* 541

Cold War (definition) *4:* 678

Collins, Michael *3:* 493

Collinson, Richard *1:* 98

Colorado River *1:*87, 88

Colson, Charles *4:* 656

Columbia River Territory *1:* 87–88

Columbia 2: 322

Columbus, Bartholomeo *1:* 19, 21

Columbus, Christopher *1:* **14–23,** 16 (ill.)

Columbus, Diego *1:* 22

Columbus, Fernando *1:* 19, 22

Comiskey, Charles *4:* 607, 610–12

Commoner, Barry *2:* 280

Communism *3:* 521–23, 527, 539, 543

Communist Party *4:* 627–29, 635, 638

Confederacy *3:* 454, 462, 463–64

Confederate States of America *3:* 446

Connally, John *4:* 656

Connolly, James *3:* 489, 491, 493

Conquistadors (definition) *1:* 24

Continental Army *3:* 406

Contras *3:* 551

Cook Strait *1:* 68

Cook, Frederick Albert *1:* **135–43,** 137 (ill.), 142 (ill.)

Cook, James *1:* **65–74,** 66 (ill.)

Cooley, Denton *2:* 215

Cooper's Creek *1:* 115, 117, 118, 120

Copper mining in Butte, Montana *2:* **191–97**

Pindar 3: 384

Pinta 1: 17

Pirie, Lord 2: 199

Pittman, Sandy Hill 1: 180, 187

Pizarro, Francisco 1: 29, 30

Plunkett, Joseph 3: 489, 493

Plutarch 4: 563, 564

Poindexter, John 3: 551

Polaris 1: 103, 129

Polay, Victor 4: 718

The Postman 4: 667

Potawototi 1: 59

Prince William Sound 2: 338, 340, 343, 344

Proctor and Gamble Company 4: 709

Project Ranch Hand 2: 275, 278

Pruss, Max 2: 224, 227, 228

Ptolemy XI 4: 561, 564

Ptolemy XIII 4: 563, 564

Ptolemy XII 4: 561, 563

Puckeshinwa 3: 409

Purity Distilling Company 2: 209, 213

Putnam, George Palmer 1: 159, 160

Q

Quintland 4: 615, 619

Quiz Show 4: 648

R

Rae, John 1: 101

Raleigh, Sir Walter 1: 40–46, 41 (ill.)

Rall, Johann Gottlieb 3: 405–06, 408

Ramotobi 1: 105

Randall, Adam 4: 692

Rao, P. V. Narasimha 2: 319

Rawlinson, Diane 4: 697, 699

Ray, Thomas (Pete) 3: 533

Raymond of Tripoli 3: 388, 391

RBMK nuclear reactor 2: 332–34, 337

Readick, Frank 4: 623

Reagan, Ronald 2: 320, 327; 3: 551-51, 553

Redford, Robert 4: 658

Redmon, Paul 4: 680

Redstone Arsenal 2: 235

Reed, James 1: 90, 94

Reed, Margaret 1: 94

Reed, Virginia 1: 93

Rehnskold, Karl Gustaf 3: 400–02, 404

Reid, Joe 1: 174,en>78

Reno, Jonet 4: 682

Reno, Marcus 3: 467

Resnick, Judith 2: 324

Resolution 1: 71,en>74

Resource Conservation and Recovery Act 2: 242

Return of the Jedi 4: 660

Reunion 4: 617

Revlon 4: 642, 643

Reynolds, Kevin 4: 665, 666

Rhee, Syngman 3: 524

Rhodes, Richard 2: 363–64

Ribicoff, Abraham 2: 269, 270

Richardson, Elliot 4: 655

Richardson-Merrel 2: 256

Risberg, Charles "Swede" 4: 608, 609

Roanoke Colony 1: 47–52, 48 (ill.)

Robards, Jason 2: 251

Robin Hood, Prince of Thieves 4: 665, 666

Rodino, Peter 4: 657

Rogers, William B. 2: 328

Rogers Commission 2: 320, 328–29

Rogovin Report 2: 300

Roosevelt, Eleanor 1: 160

Roosevelt, Franklin D. 1: 52, 135, 143; 2: 251

Rose, Pete 4: 613

The Rosenberg case 3: **633–40,** 639

Rosenberg, Ethel 4: 633, 634–40, 634 (ill.)

Rosenberg, Julius 4: 633, 634–40, 634 (ill.)

Rosenhouse, Martin 4: 643

Ross, James Clark 1: 98, 101

Ross, John 1: 100–02

Roswell Cancer Institute 2: 242

Rothstein, Arnold 4: 610–12

Routhier, Daniel 4: 617

Roxana 3: 380, 384

Royal Society 1: 65, 68, 147

Ruckelhaus, William 4: 655

Rundstedt, Karl von 3: 509

Rusk, Dean 2: 275

Russell, W. H. 3: 435

S

Safety of Life at Sea conference 2: 206

Saint–Gaudens, Augustus 3: 453

Saladin 3: 386, 389 (ill.), 390, 391

Salt Lake 1:83

Samurai 3: 512, 513

Sandwich Islands 1: 73

Santa Maria 1: 17, 18

"Saturday Night Massacre" 4: 655

Satyagraha 3: 499

Saunders, Eugene 4: 699

Sauwaseekau 3: 410, 411

Saxbe, William 4: 655

Sayles, John 4: 614

Saypol, Irving 4: 638